DATE DUE

JA 8 '95			
JA 29 '93			
JE 22 '93			
JE 22 '93			
AG 30 '93			
OC 14 '94			
DE 1 '95			
DE 17 '97			
JE 6 '07			

Second Thoughts

Second Thoughts About Race in America

Edited by

PETER COLLIER and DAVID HOROWITZ

MADISON BOOKS
Lanham • New York • London

Co-published by arrangement with
the National Forum Foundation

Published by Madison Books
4720 Boston Way
Lanham, Maryland 20706

3 Henrietta Street
London WC2E 8LU England

Distributed by National Book Network

The paper used in this publication meets the minimum requirements of American National Standard for Information Sciences—Permanence of Paper for Printed Library Materials, ANSI Z39.48–1984. ∞™
Manufactured in the United States of America.

Library of Congress Cataloging-in-Publication Data

Second Thoughts About Race in America / edited by Peter Collier and David Horowitz.
p. cm.
Proceedings of a conference held in Washington, D.C. in the spring of 1990.
Includes bibliographical references.
1. Afro-Americans—Civil rights.
2. United States—Race relations.
3. Racism—United States. 4. Civil rights movements—United States—History—20th century.
I. Collier, Peter. II. Horowitz, David, 1939- .
E185.615.S374 1991
323'.0973—dc20 91-29959 CIP
ISBN 0–8191–8243–5 (cloth. : alk. paper)

British Cataloging in Publication Information Available

Contents

III. Standards and Double Standards

IV. The New Racism and the American Dream

Acknowledgements

We are, of course, grateful to those who joined us at this conference and delivered the perceptive and courageous observations that make up this volume. There are others who were equally important in making this book happen.

We would like to express our deep appreciation to our friends Michael Joyce and Hillel Fradkin at the Harry and Lynde Bradley Foundation; Jim Capua and Bill Alpert at the William H. Donner Foundation; and Bill Simon, Jim Piereson and Bill Voegeli at the John M. Olin Foundation. Without these individuals and institutions, the intellectual landscape of this country would be more arid and monochromatic.

We are also indebted to Kim Ohnemus for her effort in helping to organize the conference; to Therese Lyons for her intelligent effort in preparing the manuscript of this book; and to Jim Denton of the National Forum Foundation for joining us in this endeavor and others we have undertaken in the last few years.

Foreword

Peter Collier

In the fall of 1987, David Horowitz and I convened what we called the Second Thoughts Conference. It was a look back in anger, or at least contentiousness, at the 1960s by a large number of one-time activists, like ourselves, who had tried to live out radical fantasies then and tried to live them down in the years that followed. This Conference and the book, *Second Thoughts*, which followed, attempted to evaluate that radical decade, and to understand how the New Left, which began with brave visions of participatory democracy, could have ended in a spasm of violence and cynicism about democratic values and about America itself.

In the midst of the obdurate anti-nostalgia of that weekend in Washington, D.C., however, there was one aspect of the 1960s that remained undiminished by revisions or admissions: the civil rights movement. Some of the participants of the Second Thoughts Conference had done work in the South at the time of Mississippi Summer; almost all considered the civil rights movement the one unalloyed achievement of an era they otherwise regarded with increasing ambivalence. Yet even here it was apparent that the destructive character of that era had had an enduring impact. All these former radicals well-remembered how Martin Luther King was supplanted by quintessential New Left figures like Stokley Carmichael, Rap Brown, and Huey Newton; and how, in the councils of pandemonium of the radical left, these rejectionists had proceeded to dismiss integration in favor of separatism, replace the patiently-sought and hard-won gain with the non-negotiable demand, and kiss off those who had struggled for racial justice for years by telling them that they had become part of the problem rather than part of the solution.

Because of the way this bitter legacy has intensified racial polarization in America today, we decided to organize another conference which would elaborate on the first one. It was called "Second Thoughts About Race," and it took place in Washington, D.C. in the spring of 1990.

The participants were individuals whose sensibilities had been shaped by the civil rights movement. They believed that the dilemma of race was a tragic and enduring stain on the American experience, but they were aware of the dramatic progress that had been made in their own lifetimes, progress that could not have been anticipated twenty-five years ago. Most of them had fought in one way or another for Martin Luther King's vision (simple-sounding, perhaps, but hard to achieve) in which people would be judged by the content of their character rather than the color of their skin. They were aware of the irony that while King devoted his life to giving America the moral force to build a colorblind society, those who had claimed his mantle had stigmatized colorblindness as the philosophy of the unenlightened.

Those who attended this Conference may have disagreed about many things. But they were all suspicious of the "politically correct" thinking that insists on identity based on race instead of individuality, demands advancement by virtue of entitlement rather than merit, and seeks to create a system of preferences, double standards, and predictable statistical outcomes which can only manufacture rather than solve racism.

What happened to civil rights? How did the concept of equal opportunity get mugged by proponents of equality of outcome? Why did the emphasis shift in the struggle for racial justice from the individual to the group? How did the term "racism," once used to define a social pathology, become a bludgeon in the hands of those who promote what George Orwell called "the smelly little orthodoxies"? Why was the civil rights leadership of the early 1960s, one of the most responsible and optimistic groups in American life, supplanted by civil rights professionals of the 1990s who propose wild conspiracy theories (AIDS is spread among blacks by Jewish doctors; the crack epidemic in the ghetto is a genocidal plot by whites) and preach dark pessimism about the American character?

In addressing these and other questions, those who spoke at this Conference knew that their deliberations would be regarded, to say the least, as controversial. But most of them were used to going against the grain. As a leader of SNCC in 1963, for instance, Julius Lester had faced intimidation in Mississippi, just as he had faced intimidation later on as a professor at the University of Massachusetts because he insisted on holding onto his old principles. Stanley Crouch's incisive and iconoclastic views on racial and other matters had rubbed *bien pensant* intellectuals of the left the wrong way throughout the 1980s. Harvard professor Glenn Loury, a black neo-conservative, had been regularly condemned for heresy since his work first started appearing in the 1970s. Journalist Joe Klein had been called a "racist" for honestly reporting on the tragic and complex truths behind the "new racism" in New York City.

For these individuals and the others whose insights comprise *Second Thoughts About Race*, appearing at this Conference was an act of courage and an act of faith as well -- faith in the power of reason and in the ability of American society to complete the journey begun in the Deep South more than three decades ago.

Proceedings of conferences are usually inert and lifeless documents, no matter how exciting the event itself may have been. *Second Thoughts on Race* is, I believe, an exception to this rule. The high quality of the dialogue shines through the pages of this book and so does the integrity of the participants -- people who have changed much over the years, but who have held steadfastly to the vision of a just and equitable society where racism, even the affirmative racism of liberal social engineers, cannot be tolerated. That views so principled and persuasive should be those of a minority is troubling. Yet it is exhilarating that there are those who are still willing, in the words of the old civil rights song, to keep their eyes on the prize and hold on.

Part 1

After Civil Rights

Julius Lester

Ronald Radosh

Richard Cohen

Fredrick Robinson

Walter Williams

Juan Williams

Joe Klein

1

Whatever Happened to the Civil Rights Movement

Julius Lester

In its essence, the civil rights movement brought reality to the rhetoric of the democratic ideal of "freedom and justice for all." How could the United States present itself as being the "land of the free" if ten percent of its population was a racial group systematically denied basic constitutional rights, rights involving free and unhampered access to public accommodations, housing, education, and, most fundamental of all from a civic point of view, the right to vote.

However, there is another side to the meaning of the civil rights movement. While endeavouring to persuade America to live up to its constitutional principles, the civil rights movement also challenged one of those principles, a principle that remains with us though the language in which it is cast today differs from that of 35 years ago.

The civil rights movement forced the nation to wrestle with the issue of states' rights vs. federal rights. How was the federal government to respond when a group of states insisted on enforcing laws that were in clear violation of the nation's Constitution? The conservative position, then as now, was that the less power which resided in the federal government and the more reserved for state and local governments, the stronger the democracy. This is an admirable principle which articulates a certain truth to safeguard the nation from even inadvertently slipping into a condition of governmental tyranny.

However, the sad reality was that ten percent of the population was being subjected to social, economic, and political tyranny by the system of racial segregation and racial disenfranchisement.

It would be well for conservatives to be prudent and judicious in their critiques of the liberals and radicals who made the civil rights movement to remember that those liberals and radicals were reacting against a conservatism that opposed the civil rights movement, not because conservatives were racist by definition, but because conservatives gave the appearance, at least, of championing the principle of states' rights over the principle of "freedom and justice for all."

The civil rights movement came into being to correct a fundamental injustice and the final truth is that the civil rights movement was victorious.

Thus, the first thing that happened to the civil rights movement was that it won. It had set out in the mid-'50s to change the apartheid system of racial segregation in public places. With the passage of the 1964 Civil Rights Act, that was accomplished. In the early '60s, the movement set out to ensure that blacks had access to the voting booth. With the passage of the 1965 Voting Rights Act, that was accomplished. Much still needed to be done to implement and enforce these acts, but the legal principle of "freedom and justice for all" had been reiterated and given a new formulation in law.

The civil rights movement was not only successful in achieving its goals, the movement did something unprecedented in American history. It brought tens of thousands of blacks and whites together to work for the common good.

The impression is given today that the civil rights movement was a black movement. It was not. It was an integrated movement and innumerable whites also risked their lives and sanity for the principle of "freedom and justice for all." Innumerable whites carry wounds, psychological and physical, their legacy of the days and months of living in the valley of the shadow of death.

It is startling to remember the integrated nature of the movement, its self-conscious and unself-conscious reaching across cultural and class differences to learn from and with each other. It is startling to remember that period when today blacks and whites are more separated than ever and the only bridge linking the two is mutual suspicion and animosity.

But one must be careful to not romanticize or idealize the civil rights movement because it did not represent the totality of the black political reality in the '60s. The movement's southern locale and ethos, as well as its religious underpinnings that gave non-violence a coherent context, separated it from the angrier mood being expressed simultaneously by northern blacks.

The summer President Lyndon Johnson signed the Civil Rights Act was also the first of what came to be known as "the long hot summers" when northern blacks clashed with police and burned buildings in urban areas. From 1964 to 1968, it was common to turn on one's television and see the news photos of smoke rising over an American city, smoke from the fire of a black despair, anger, and frustration that seemed to say that the Civil Rights Act of 1964 and the Voting Rights Act of 1965 were too little, too late.

I was in Hattiesburg, Mississippi, that summer of 1964 when Lyndon Johnson signed the Civil Rights Act. It was July 2. Goodman, Schwerner, and Chaney had been missing for two weeks. Those of us in "the movement" knew they were dead. We did not celebrate the signing of the Civil Rights Act. How could we?

What also happened to the civil rights movement, then, is that it was affected by the conditions of blacks in the North where the problems were not as easily identifiable as the segregation and denial of voting rights in the South.

In its attempt to respond to the angrier northern black mood, the civil rights movement stepped over the line separating the politically possible from the politically impossible. It ventured into political utopianism, an emotional exaggeration which said that an America that was less than heaven on earth was to be denigrated as less than any nation on earth.

This expression of frustration is understandable because civil rights is a limited concept whose aim is to ensure those rights guaranteed to citizens under the Constitution. What those rights are and how the Constitution is interpreted are not always clear and that is part of the messiness of democracy. The very messiness of democracy is one of its overriding strengths. Civil rights is concerned with the possible.

In the mid-'60s the civil rights movement shifted from the possible to the impossible, a move characterized by a change from civil rights to something called human rights.

The formulation appears first in the speeches of Malcolm X, where he makes the following rather simplistic distinction: "Civil rights is domestic. Human rights is international."[1]

[1] **By Any Means Necessary** by Malcolm X; Pathfinder Press (1970), p.20.

This distinction was adopted by James Forman, one of the leaders of the Student Non-Violent Coordinating Committee. He persuaded the organization to declare itself a "human rights organization working for the liberation not only of black people in the United States but of all oppressed peoples, especially those in Africa, Asia and Latin America."[2]

The summer of 1967 Forman spoke before the International Seminar on Apartheid, Racism, and Colonialism in Southern Africa, a United Nations sponsored conference held in Ritwe, Zambia. There he elaborated on what he meant by human rights:

> We see the worldwide fight against racism as indivisible....SNCC is dedicated to a joint struggle of all who fight for Human Rights in Africa and in the U.S.A., each backing up the other, each rendering what support it can to the other....
>
> The fight against racism is a responsibility of all who believe in Human Rights, but it is the victims who bear primary responsibility for waging struggle.

Suddenly, political energy was not to be organized and focused on ensuring constitutionally guaranteed rights. Attention was shifted to racism and human rights, and we begin the journey into the nightmare of black-white relations today.

Three words Forman uses should be looked at to better understand what happened to civil rights: *racism*, *human rights*, and *victims*. They are still "buzz words" designed to make blacks feel self-righteously indignant over real and imagined wrongs, designed to make whites feel eternally guilty as the perpetrators of those wrongs. What is involved, however, are very fundamental distinctions between public and private, and the poisoning of the public arena with private demons.

Let me illustrate: As a believer in the Constitution and the First Amendment, I defend the right of any person in this country to be a bigot -- in his or her house, private club, fraternity, organization, etc. I have my prejudices. Some of them I have become quite fond of and attached to, and in the privacy of my domicile, I indulge these prejudices when the occasion arises. However, when I leave my home and enter the public sphere, there are ways in which I am no longer permitted to be a private person. When I leave my home, I become a citizen and it is expected and assumed that my public behavior corresponds to that expected of all citizens.

---

[2] **The Making of Black Revolutionaries** by James Forman; MacMillan (1972), p. 480.

Therefore, racism is an issue in the public domain to the extent that it violates my rights as a citizen. America is still in the midst of trying to determine how we ascertain when that has occurred. This is much of what lies at the center of the debates on affirmative action.

When Forman proposed an international fight against racism, he said, in effect, that the opinions, feelings, and prejudices of private individuals were legitimate targets of political action. This was dangerous in the extreme, because such a formulation is merely a new statement of totalitarianism, the effort to control not only the behavior of citizens but the thoughts and feelings of persons.

What I think, what I feel can never be the concern of government. If I do not like that someone gets up in public and espouses racism or anti-Semitism, then, for democracy's sake, my response should be to stand up and put forward countering ideas and persuade more people to my ideals of community, democracy, etc., than my adversary can persuade to his ideal of bigotry. The simultaneous strength and danger of democracy is that it is an arena in which we are willing to take the risk that the worst idea can win.

I prefer that risk to the arrogance of those who think it is the responsibility of the schools to involve themselves in teaching children not to be racists, who are foisting onto the schools something called "multi-cultural" education. The cultural education of a child is not the responsibility of government. If Hispanics, blacks, Cambodians, Vietnamese, etc., want their children to know their respective cultures, that is the responsibility of those respective communities. It is the responsibility of the schools to take the Hispanic, black, white, Cambodian, Vietnamese children and say, "Each of you comes from a different culture, but beyond that cultural identity, there is another one, and that is that we are all American citizens, and here are the concepts, ideals, experiences, hopes, and dreams which bind us together as Americans."

The shift from fighting for civil rights to fighting against racism was a shift from seeking and finding the common ground to a position which has been disastrously divisive. To fight against racism divides humanity into an "us against them" situation. It leads to a self-definition as "victim" such that anyone who defines himself as a victim has found a way to keep himself in a perpetual state of righteous self-pity and anger, and that, in a nutshell, is the state of much of black America today.

It is a pathetic litany that pours unceasingly from the mouths of many blacks daily and has led to surrealistic absurdities. When the mayor of Washington, D.C. is arrested on a charge of possession and use of cocaine and the head of the National Association for the Advancement of Colored People says that the mayor is a victim of government harassment, we have entered a Kafkaesque world in which agreement on what is reality is no longer possible. When that same mayor is given a standing ovation at the National Black Mayor's conference, when the black community at large sees the mayor as a victim of "Whitey" and refuses to consider the possibility that the mayor has abused his office and moral responsibility as an elected official, we have entered an era when many blacks have not only lost any semblance of what is acceptable behavior and what is not, they have reached a point at which they don't even seem to care, and that is most distressing of all.

The most dangerous aspect of this formulation of human rights as the struggle of victims against racism is the distorting of what is meant by rights. In the Constitution the most basic right is the right to be free from governmental interference. Nowhere is a right construed as a privilege of the individual. Civil rights means, therefore, that the government will not interfere in certain areas, and in later amendments that the government will enforce the citizen's right to be treated as a citizen.

Therefore, one does not have the right not to be bothered by racism. It would be nice. It is certainly desirable. But the fact remains, there is no right to be free from racism, anti-Semitism, or sexism.

What has happened is that the phrase "human rights" has come to be used to justify anything that anyone wants. One hears that a woman has a "right" to an abortion. That is not so. One hears that the "rights" of the unborn must be protected. That is not so. The "unborn" are not citizens. I am not certain that anyone has something called "the right-to-life." Given the number of spontaneous abortions and miscarriages that occur in nature, I know that my own life is a glorious accident of nature because I have no other way of understanding why I was born and why I survived and so many other fetuses did not.

Once again, issues that belong to the person have been thrust into the public arena and the society is being asked to codify matters I am not sure are susceptible to codification. The latest of these is the so-called "Right to Die" issue. We are asking the legal system to determine when life begins and when it ends. The most the legal system can do adequately is determine what we cannot do to another in the conduct of our public affairs if we are to have a cohesive society. All matters beyond that are more properly determined in the arena of public opinion which ebbs and flows considerably before consensus is arrived at mysteriously.

The civil rights movement then was, in reality, much broader than the specific issues of access to public accommodations, education, employment, and the voting booth. The civil rights movement involved fundamental questions of relations between federal and state and local governments, as well as issues of private and public, of personhood and citizenship.

What happened to the civil rights movement is that it abdicated responsibility for the society as a whole and opted for the sloth of blacks being eternal victims who want to lay claims on the emotions and sympathies of others, who no longer are aware of or even care to work toward something that might be agreed upon as the common good but, instead, focus exclusively upon their own concerns as if there were no others that also demand the nation's legitimate attention.

What happened to the civil rights movement is what can happen to any political movement, conservative or liberal, which is that one grows weary of the chaotic maelstrom that democracy can be, that one gets impatient with the complex process required for change on a societal scale, that one becomes intolerant and scornful of those with whom one disagrees, and most dangerous of all, that one begins to assert that his or her particular truth is really the truth. Ironically, sometimes, that might very well be so. But to act toward others as if it is so is to divide the world, yet again, into an "us against them."

As we look at America today, we should see and not only be horrified but also weary from the effects of an "us against them" mentality. Black and white do not speak to each other anymore. They live in camps of the eternally vigilant, one against the other. They have lost any semblance of knowing that there is something beyond being black and being white; there is the fact that we are Americans. That is not a call to patriotism or nationalism. It is a call to recognize each other as citizens and to come together as citizens to understand what we share as citizens.

2

From Civil Rights to Black Power: The Breakup of the Civil Rights Coaltion

Ronald Radosh

When James Meredith was shot in 1966, as he sought to march from Memphis, Tennessee, to Jackson, Mississippi, the black civil rights activists who took his place to complete his journey showed a new face to the country at large. As Martin Luther King, Jr. had espoused non-violence and his followers had chanted "Freedom Now," Stokely Carmichael and other SNCC militants now called for power, and urged that blacks respond to white terror in kind. Their approach was reflected in the slogan "Black Power!," which, as Julius Lester reminded us, was "gonna get your momma." In the coming era of polarization, the works of Frantz Fanon replaced those of Albert Camus as the popular theoretical guide in the Movement. It was inevitable that an early veteran of SNCC like John Lewis would quietly resign from the organization to which he had given so much. The time for Lewis' kind of message was over.

In chanting Black Power, the Movement had done more than echo the frustration and anger of scores of Southern blacks, understandably tired of the terror in their own communities and the struggle for change which seemed to take so long. For the hope of national and local change, as King and Bayard Rustin had so effectively argued, was in a national coalition including whites, particularly those from the labor movement and liberal groups whose interests coincided with that of the black population, which composed 11 percent of the population. How correct was Bayard Rustin, when he wrote in his seminal *Commentary* article that the militants of SNCC had a position that was simultaneously "utopian and reactionary;" since one-tenth of the population could not accomplish much by itself, and because their stance of Black Power would remove American blacks from the main area of political struggle and give priority to the issue of race, when the fundamental issues facing America were economic and social.

Rustin's plea fell on deaf ears. These divisions first came to attention at the Atlantic City 1964 Democratic convention, when the Mississippi Freedom Democratic Party waged a struggle to obtain the seats of the regular, all-white Democratic Party of Senator James Eastland. Concerned with white Southern support in the race, the Johnson White House advanced a compromise that it sought to have the MFDP adopt that would have allowed the Democratic Party regulars from Mississippi to hold on to their seats while granting token representation to only two MFDP delegates.

There is a mythology about this event, which has by now seeped into virtually every scholarly account of the civil rights movement. The myth asserts that because of the compromise proposed by the White House, the white liberal/labor coalition -- more anxious to maintain its ties to the White House and hoping for a Hubert Humphrey vice presidential appointment -- sided with the racists and supported the compromise. As a result, Garry Wills wrote in the first version of this myth, "disillusioned kids, blacks from the S.N.C.C. and white workers from the South began to form a new constituency," one seeking to "enlighten the Movement" rather than to play the old coalition politics.

Black Power, as well as the subsequent New Left subordination to black revolutionaries, has thus been laid at the hands of the sellout orchestrated by Joe Rauh, Walter Reuther, and Bayard Rustin in 1964. As a result, supposedly, the New Left was born.

The truth, as Joe Rauh put it, was that the MFDP achieved a success "far beyond anything that could have reasonably have been anticipated a month or two earlier." Their struggle led to the Voting Rights Act of 1965, drove the racist regulars from future Democratic conventions, and gave blacks in Mississippi a legitimacy previously denied them. They also had won recognition for the need for reform in the delegate selection process. 1964, in retrospect, marked the end of white power in the Democratic Party in the deep South. It is no wonder that most Mississippi blacks sought eventually to work within the Democratic Party and to rebuild it along interracial lines, in alliance with white liberals, mainstream civil rights groups, and moderates from the ranks of organized labor.

Referring to the New Left mythology, Joe Rauh has commented that "there was no sell-out or double-dealing." Writing to Wills, Rauh commented that the "New Left must be in a helluva shape when it has to fabricate the reasons for its existence." Not only had Rauh and his liberal allies fought to the bitter end for the full seating of the MFDP, Rauh noted that contrary to what SNCC militants were saying, even Bob Moses first favored the compromise, until pressure from within SNCC forced him to give in.

The message offered by SNCC militants was that stated bluntly by Carmichael, that Atlantic City showed the black freedom movement "could not rely on their so-called allies." The liberals, James Forman later wrote, wanted to "sell out the people." Ignored was the firm advice of Rustin, who continually reiterated that moving from protest to politics meant the necessity of compromise; to win small victories and then return for more. As Rustin made his presentation to civil rights workers gathered at a black church in Atlantic City, the very first response he got was one which was to typify much of what would later come from the white New Left. Rising to his feet, a white Jewish SNCC worker from Atlanta got up and shouted: "You're a traitor, Bayard, a traitor."

Before long, that same SNCC worker and others of his self-sacrificing comrades would be expelled from the organization, told that the work of black liberation was to be carried out by blacks alone. America, as Charles Sherrod said in 1964, was a country of racists which demanded only "naked confrontation." As part of that confrontation, SNCC and other militants made a new coalition -- with Old Leftists and American Communists, who in their eyes were the only forces untainted with racism. From the beginning, leaders like Ella Baker argued that the black movement had to break with the liberal/labor coalition. When Rauh spoke in opposition to that line, he recalled that Baker "cut me to ribbons as an appeaser in terms I had not heard since our debates with the Henry Wallace people back in 1948." To militants like Forman, all this was beside the point. He was not going to have those who were going to risk their lives taking advice from intellectuals in "a comfortable setting in Greenwich Village or New York's Upper West Side telling them 'you're soft on communism.'" Seeing Communists simply as "progressives," Forman attacked what he called "Red-baiting by liberals." And Forman attacked Rustin's views as the false advice of those hewing to a "social-democratic line."

A scant two years after Atlantic City, the polarization had become complete. Black activists had moved towards espousal of armed rebellion, black nationalism and other forms of revolutionary posturing, including regular attacks on those within the Movement who favored an alliance with whites for social change. Whites who once worked with SNCC had moved on to white student organizations like SDS. These organizations became a network of white support for black militants, willingly subordinate to them. Unconditional solidarity with black activists became the *sine qua non* of white leftist commitment.

Perhaps nowhere was this shown better than at the 1967 "New Politics" convention held in Chicago -- called as an attempt by the white peace forces to develop a new politics of protest in opposition to the Vietnam policy of the Johnson administration. At first, the delegates hoped for creation of a new third party ticket -- a dream ticket headed by King with Ben Spock as his running mate, which would symbolize the unity of the white anti-war movement with that of the civil rights movement. The event, however, was to prove something far different.

Just as young black militants became intoxicated with the vision of taking power into their own hands, white New Leftists saw subordination to the black struggle as the path towards revolution. Blacks at home became the surrogate proletariat; the internal Third World in which lay the only remaining hope for revolution. The Chicago Conference for a New Politics, held at the revolutionary Palmer House Grand Ballroom, was to mark the fusion of the white New Left and the black liberation movements. The tension was apparent from the start. As King delivered his keynote and called for a new coalition of conscience, based on nonviolence, militants marched outside the ballroom, chanting "Kill Whitey!" Then, 2100 delegates turned the event into a numbing charade of revolutionary politics.

The event started with hope. Most white liberals went convinced, as SANE's Political Action Director Sanford Gottlieb put it, that creating "a serious, responsible radical Left could benefit the United States by offering the country some new perspectives and by moving the political spectrum slightly leftward," although Gottlieb had personal doubts that "such a Left could be established by the potpourri of invited groups." Before long, Gottlieb found that most of the some 2,117 delegates representing 372 different groups were radicals who "rejected working through the established institutions of American society." Instead of liberals, the meeting, he reported, was filled with "white middle-class radicals with guilt feelings about Negroes."

Indeed, what they found was that the black radicals quickly formed their own all-black caucus, made up of members of SNCC, CORE, SCLC, Socialist Workers Party, Communist Party, and individual militants, who chose the then unknown Carlos Russell, a Panamanian-born Brooklyn social worker, as their chief spokesman. (Today, Russell is most known for his outspoken defense of Idi Amin and Manuel Noriega, both of whom he has hailed as people's leaders.) The caucus, the reporter for *The Nation* magazine wrote, was "meeting continuously in secrecy, with shaven headed bodyguards posted at the doors, shifting from one building and one room to another, staring fiercely at whites as they walked past them in hallways, and taunting them as they solicited contributions for 'our black brothers' in the jails."

The black caucus, evidently divided internally, began by demanding its own meeting room and its own structure. Its members were beholden only to the majority of the caucus, not to the entire convention. Deadlocked between blacks who wanted to participate in the convention and those who did not, the competing groups finally agreed on a strategy, as white activist and founder of the Marxist-oriented Institute for Policy Studies, Arthur Waskow put it, of discharging "their energy upon the white convention."

That took the form of what Waskow called "the toughest criteria" they could devise. If the whites accepted the test, they would stay; if they refused, the black caucus would leave. The test was the insistence that the assembled whites accept a 13 point program -- including acceptance of a black armed militia, the right of blacks to revolt when they deemed it necessary, and a dialogue for partitioning the United States into two separate nations, one black and one white. It also included a resolution condemning the Israeli victory in the six day war with Egypt, what the resolution called the "imperialistic Zionist war." That resolution was particularly aimed at Jews, who had been in the forefront of the original civil rights coalition. Instead of discussing this, the white majority quickly accepted "their own responsibility for centuries of oppression," and by a three to one margin, voted to approve all of the black demands. As one Jewish leftist screamed at a caucus meeting, "After 400 years of slavery, it is right that whites should be castrated!"

Treating themselves to a standing ovation for this action, they found that the blacks also demanded half of the convention votes. This was necessary, they said, to establish trust. As a result, one-third of the delegates present had obtained total control. An Ann Arbor white delegate explained: "We are just a little tail on the end of the very powerful black panther," While Bert Gaskoff said, "and I want to be on that tail -- if they'll let me." "Whites," he continued, "must trust the blacks the way you trust children," immediately adding "I don't mean to say it like that...these are very sophisticated people and they've taught the whites a hell of a lot." Then, two to one, the whites voted to hand full power to the black caucus.

Liberals, as Waskow approvingly wrote, had "voted to castrate themselves as organizers...because they accepted the responsibility and guilt of American racism." Of course, the ploy failed to work. Expecting to find that they would now be absolved of all sin, the white delegates found instead that the black delegates responded by storming out, proclaiming that whites had proved they were unfit to be partners with blacks in any coalition. The new revolutionary Black Power advocates had no room for working with whites, even those who swallowed all of their nonsense. The Movement was well on the road to the impasse it now faces.

Blacks had decided to go it alone, and as James Forman put it to the delegates, "anyone who doesn't like it can go to hell." "Otherwise," he added, "the liberal-labor treachery will recur." And of course, working with the New Radicals did not lead, as liberals like Gottlieb had hoped, to "increased mutual understanding" and work on "common interests." In retrospect, as Fred Siegel has noted, Black Power was "the social therapy of self-assertion," a declaration of independence from traditional coalition politics. "We don't need white liberals," Carmichael intoned. While radical in rhetoric, Black Power proved all too compatible with white corporate and liberal interests. The Ford Foundation became a major funder of Black Power projects, such as that of decentralization of the New York school system. Thus, Siegel writes, was "the momentum of a great social movement dissipated by pretension, nationalist fantasies, and a thinly disguised paternalism." Black Power, which promised so much, became a source of the unraveling of the Great Society. Once reform currents were diverted into black-only channels, the popular basis of any support for social change was undercut.

Gerald Ford had made the point clear, when he said in the Republican campaign of '68: "How long are we going to abdicate law and order -- the backbone of civilization -- in favor of a social theory that the man who heaves a brick through your window is simply the misunderstood and under-privileged product of a broken home?" Ford's rhetoric won the Republicans support from white ethnics, angry at riots in the urban centers which produced grants to black activists and only disdain for them. But it was the Black Power conference syndrome: the new tendency of white activist reformers to rationalize and support any and every black demand, however foolish, that divided the Democratic Party and began the urban ethnic shift to the Republican Party. The gap between the New Politics white liberals from the Stevenson tradition and the bread and butter old FDR Democrats had been created, and was growing wider day by day. The would-be revolutionary Black Power forces had succeeded in providing the very ammunition for the Reagan Republicans whose arrival on the scene they would soon be regularly bemoaning.

3

Nixon's The One

Richard Cohen

You may ask what a nice liberal like me is doing in a place like this. I really don't have a lot of second thoughts about the civil rights era, but I do have some additional thoughts. These occurred to me last summer when I was sitting out on the beach in Long Island reading an advance copy of the second volume of Stephen Ambrose's Richard Nixon biography. At the same time, I was looking at the newspapers from the New York area reading about the Bensonhurst killing and everything else that was happening in the country, a lot of which would seem to be about race.

I was working on a couple of pieces about the 1988 election and reading this book and sort of saying to myself, well, not a lot has changed in this country. Back in 1968 Richard Nixon ran against the city of Washington, calling it the crime capital of the United States. At that time it didn't deserve the title, but it has since earned it under three Republican presidents, all of whom promised to do something about it.

Richard Nixon campaigned against crime in general. So did George Bush. Richard Nixon campaigned against forced integration or forced busing. But by the time George Bush came along, that was no longer an issue. But most of the issues haven't changed, and the country seemed to not have gotten 'off the dime' when it comes to race. Indeed, race has been our abiding problem in the United States ever since slavery. We haven't really come to grips with it.

I was reading the Ambrose book and thinking about Richard Nixon and where this all began, because Richard Nixon was the architect of the so-called southern strategy. It was interesting to listen to what Ron Radosh had to say because I'm going to talk a little bit about the same era, the same issues. For my part, I don't particularly blame the left and what is now certainly the cuckoo wing of the civil rights movement for what happened politically in this country. It seems to me that those people in the center and to the right are at least as responsible as those people who were throwing bricks through the windows.

But first let me go back to the 1972 campaign because at that time busing was an issue, as were various kinds of desegregation efforts, and Richard Nixon was campaigning vociferously against them. Nixon's attitude publicly stated was that forced busing, as it used to be called, was wrong, that he wouldn't condone it, he wouldn't put up with it. He never quite explained how it was that his own Justice Department was insisting on it.

But as Reagan later did, Nixon developed a posture of sort of running against his own government. He was not responsible somehow for the law. He was not responsible for the various suits brought by the Justice Department. He was responsible, though, for trying to assemble the coalition that has since become a core of the Republican Party, of disaffected whites in the South and what we loosely call urban ethnics in the North. He was eminently successful in doing that.

Nixon's attitude about civil rights and desegregation can probably best be described or characterized by a memo he wrote to his trusty sidekick John Ehrlichman, who later had good opportunity to study these issues in the clink. Nixon summed it up by saying: "Legally segregated education, legally segregated housing, legal obstruction to equal employment must be totally removed. On the other hand, while I am convinced that legal segregation is totally wrong, forced education, forced desegregation of housing or education is just as wrong." I'm not sure what kind of message this is except that to me it says that on the one hand it's wrong to segregate a public facility, and on the other hand it's just as wrong to forcibly desegregate that public facility.

And that is precisely, or approximately (depending on how you look at it) the posture Richard Nixon struck during that campaign. He never bothered to explain why the Justice Department was bringing suit after suit in various school districts in the South. He never bothered to explain what the differences were, legally and semantically, between integration and desegregation. He never bothered to blame school districts that persistently broke the law by maintaining segregated facilities throughout the South and in some cases in the North. He never said anything about school boards that built schools and arranged boundaries to perpetuate segregated education.

Instead, he talked only about forced busing and how bad it was.

Now, maybe in America all that is excused when it comes to politics. I mean, after all, if you don't win, you're nowhere and winning is everything, losing is whatever it is. I can trot out all the cliches; you know them.

The trouble for Richard Nixon in 1972 was that for a while he faced a potential threat from his right in the name of George Wallace. Wallace was the governor of Alabama and was running as a Democrat in the primaries. But there was a lot of thought at the time that he might run as an independent in the general election and siphon off votes and throw the election to the Democrats.

By July or August, however, it was clear that George Wallace was not going to do anything of the sort.

Richard Nixon's opponent in 1972, you will remember, was one George McGovern. By the convention itself, George McGovern was dead in the water. You have to recall that on the night that he accepted the nomination of the Democratic Party, 33 nominations were made for vice president, including ones for Martha Mitchell and Mao Tse Tung. In the end, McGovern did even worse -- he chose Eagleton and by the end of the week Jack Anderson had broken a story that Eagleton had undergone electric shock therapy because he had been depressed. Eagleton was then dumped from the ticket and a number of people turned down the offer of the vice presidency, and McGovern wound up with Sargent Shriver.

By August the election was over. In the end Richard Nixon won every state but one. That was Massachusetts. He compiled the greatest landslide in Republican history. He did better even than Dwight Eisenhower. At no time, given the edge that he had, given the absolute certainty that he was going to win this election, did Richard Nixon ever pause and try to explain why the Justice Department was doing what it was doing, what the plight of blacks was in the South, what the law of the land was. At no time in this election did Richard Nixon ever pause to try to bring the country together, to try to reconcile the divergent groups in the country and explain what was happening.

Instead, he attacked, attacked, attacked.

That pattern has not been broken by the Republican Party since. Nixon is vindicated in the sense that he did assemble the coalition that he wanted to assemble. We have it still in existence today.

Jerry Ford, who didn't like people throwing bricks through the windows, nevertheless campaigned in the manner of Richard Nixon.

Ronald Reagan, of course, did it, and did it to an extraordinary degree.

George Bush, in the last campaign, did somewhat the same thing, once again catering to disaffected whites in the South, urban ethnics in the North, keeping that Republican coalition together.

Now, whatever you may call that coalition, and there are various terms for it, it is essentially this: it is anti-black. These people may be paranoid about blacks, they may be afraid of blacks, they may hate blacks, whatever the case may be. The single issue that drives them -- or drove them -- into the Republican Party is a feeling about race. This is true particularly, and significantly, in the North where various so-called urban ethnics have gone over to the Republican Party. I can only think of Frank Rizzo. I don't think it was anyone's intellectual position or the papers coming out of the Heritage Foundation that got Rizzo to change his registration to the Republican Party.

When I look back at the 1988 election, even if I manage to forget for a second Willie Horton and what that ugly, ugly campaign represented, if I just look at the results of that election, it's very depressing. George Bush won, as we all know. He got approximately 12 percent of the black vote.

Blacks now are in the Democratic Party almost 100 percent in Presidential elections. At the time that Richard Nixon began his political career, that was not the case. You need only recall that Martin Luther King and his father were nominal Republicans, and in the early days looked to the Republican Party and figures such as Nelson Rockefeller to do something about civil rights and to advance the cause of blacks. I don't think many blacks in this country look to the Republican Party that way anymore. They have in a sense been told, whether it is literally true or not, that they're not welcome in this party.

When I looked at the results of the 1988 election after the election itself, I found a pattern that I thought was very disturbing, and that was this: the smaller the proportion of blacks in a given state, the greater the chance that it would have voted for Michael Dukakis and not for George Bush. In fact, nine of the ten states that went for Michael Dukakis -- New York was the only exception -- had considerably fewer blacks percentage-wise than the nation as a whole, and much fewer than states like Mississippi or Texas or southern states which have a considerable number of blacks.

An interesting state to look at is Oregon. Oregon went 53 to 47 for Dukakis. What's interesting in Oregon and it happens again in some of the other states that went to Dukakis is that not only did Dukakis get the black vote, but he got the majority of the white vote. This was almost never the case elsewhere in the country. With the exception again of New York, you'll find the same pattern for Iowa, Minnesota, West Virginia, Hawaii, Washington, Rhode Island, Wisconsin, and even Massachusetts. In West Virginia we find something else as well. Not only did Dukakis get a majority of the white vote -- 53 percent -- but Bush got 29 percent of the black vote. Nationally, he got only 12 percent.

The pattern seems to be that wherever there are large numbers of blacks, you have racial polarization along political lines. Where there are insignificant numbers of blacks, then both blacks and whites vote differently than they do elsewhere.

Okay. People have said to me, yeah, sure. But where there are large numbers of blacks there is a fear of crime. There is a great deal of tension. There's hostility. There's the kind of tabloid sensationalism you get in New York after incidents like Howard Beach and Bensonhurst, and the Central Park jogger case -- they go on and on like that. And that's probably true.

But the question I have is: why should one party become the party of blacks and the other of whites? And why is it that the party of whites is the party of whites who are fearful of blacks or who have antipathy toward blacks? And the reason, I think, has not so much to do -- or, as Ron Radosh said, not entirely to do -- with what went on in the days of rage in Chicago or with this caucus throwing out these people or that statement, but with the policies, the political strategies developed early on by Richard Nixon both in 1968, but particularly in 1972. And to my way of thinking, the consequences have been awful. Not only, I think, has this political polarization exacerbated the racial division in the society at large, but it means that there is simply no constituency in the Republican Party that is willing to support programs that would help poor blacks or what is generally called the underclass. It means, in the particular case of George Bush, who followed Richard Nixon's political strategy, that there is simply no constituency in his own party to support the programs that I think he himself would like to implement if he had the guts to raise taxes a little bit. It means, in this case, that the party of Lincoln, the party that blacks looked to for so long, is now the party that they've essentially turned their backs on, and it means that when people get together to discuss racial progress or civil rights or whatever you want to call it, it's really essentially a dialogue within the Democratic Party and it's often one polluted by charges of racism. It means, I think, that the country really hasn't moved very far since the civil rights era and one of the reasons it hasn't moved very far, significantly, I think, is because of the policies adopted by Richard Nixon in the early 1970s and followed by national Republican political candidates ever since.

Usually, when Richard Nixon is discussed, someone says that he was a great foreign policy President but not so great a President on domestic policy. I think, though, if you look at the racial polarization in the country today, you have to reach a different conclusion. I think he was a disaster.

4

My Second Thoughts

Fredrick D. Robinson

I was born during the heyday of the civil rights movement when a generation of blacks were in the streets fighting for civil and human rights -- one year before the death of Malcolm X and three years before Dr. King was gunned down on the balcony of an Alabama hotel. Growing up in an apolitical family, I was too young and too sheltered to experience the virulent conflicts of the decade of political protests and mass demonstrations. Even though I was cognizant of the shameful history of American slavery, Jim Crow, and segregation, I had a child-like innocence about race relations. Sure, I had seen the public television documentaries of the civil rights years that recounted the courageous sacrifices of Robert Moses; Chaney, Goodman, and Schwerner; Fannie Lou Hammer; James Farmer; the Reverend Fred Shuttleworth; Dr. King; and Malcolm X. But the most ominous aspects of racism seemed relegated to some wicked past.

My "radicalism" didn't come until the early '80s when I began reading the protest fiction of Richard Wright and the angry, mesmerizing essays of James Baldwin. But, more than any other work written during the '60s, Eldridge Cleaver's poignant essay of rationalized hatred, *Soul on Ice*, turned me into a political animal. *Soul on Ice* was the impetus for my disillusionment with Capitalism, and my abhorrhence of Corporate America. To me, America was the epitome of political and social insanity as she ruthlessly oppressed her black brethren while cynically posturing as a free nation.

I was told that the reason that blacks were more likely to be incarcerated, unemployed, lacking in education, addicted to drugs, and daunted by a host of other ills was persistent racism, pure and simple. Like most young blacks who inherited too much of an earlier generation's anger, I was certain that when black people failed it was whites who were culpable.

My first essays as a young writer were fueled by what Jean-Paul Sartre called "anti-racist racism." In addition to painting blacks as morally superior to whites, I exalted communal African culture and traditions, and scorned Western mores and etiquettes. My polemical exercises intellectualized black innocence and theorized our entitlement to various government supports: affirmative action, quotas, anti-poverty programs, and civil rights.

I went even further. In strident essays I wrote that blacks could never achieve any meaningful success in America as it presently existed. Sure, there was a growing black petite bourgeoisie, but the black masses remained mired in poverty and degradation. While I supported government aid to the black community, I considered it an insulting form of charity and doubted its efficacy. I embraced Oscar Wilde's dictum: "Charity creates a multitude of sins...the proper aim is to try to reconstruct society on such a basis that poverty will be impossible." Consequently, I began to see Socialism as an instrument of salvation for blacks and oppressed people in America.

My engagement with Socialism was short-lived, however, as I distrusted its disregard for human nature. And I found Marx's metaphysical assumptions about the inevitability of a classless society closer to mysticism than to science. But for a while I remained convinced that only through some form of Socialism could mankind be saved from war, hunger, and the continued destruction of millions and millions of people, particularly non-whites.

However, the more I played with radicalism, the more disillusioned I became, particularly as I watched a generation of black thugs make the lives of fellow blacks miserable. The naive theories of the political Left -- which I glibly accepted -- began to crumble under the weight of the reality around me. The sordid rise in drug abuse, in teen pregnancies; the soaring rates of high school dropouts; the flight from educational and employment opportunities, even among middle class blacks; and the frightening conspiracy of silence among black intellectuals, first about the existence and then about the nature of these problems -- shook me out of my intellectual sloth.

Many of us eager exponents of the gospel according to the Left were so fascinated with sociology and "media images" that we overlooked the irresponsibility of our own rhetoric. It's a wonder that with all the talk about "racism," "dead-end jobs," and the "lack of real opportunities" from the pundits of the Left that there are any blacks who are still willing to get an education or to participate in mainstream society.

The '80s was the golden age of self-exaltation -- when the "don't blame us, we're the victims" syndrome reached its zenith. I remember talking to a young Marxist, a personal friend who had recently graduated from Harvard. We debated whether the destructive behavior among many blacks was attributable to their own irresponsiblity or to their environment. Her response -- a combination of pessimism, Hegel's dialectic, and hard determinism -- was that blacks who commit heinous acts of murder, participate in gang violence and in the peddling of drugs were in no way commiting acts of self-destruction. A classic determinist, she argued nihilistically that such aberrations were the inevitable result of environmental circumstances. There was no such thing as free-will.

The mechanism of self-defeat in this type of reasoning is all too clear, but liberals and radicals continue, in the name of "compassion," to propagate the idea to young blacks that they can do nothing for themselves -- and that indeed even "justifiable" and wanton criminal acts are part of nature's course.

This is the tragedy of the post-civil rights movement. As well-meaning but misguided liberals continue to wrap their narrow arms of paternalism around the black community, the result is always a pernicious abdication of responsibility and self-reliance on the part of the beneficiary. The struggle and drive for a better life, which was so much a part of earlier generations of American blacks, is continuing to evaporate in many inner-city neighborhoods as blacks become wards of the government, wedded to their status as America's historical victims.

When I was growing up, many of my fellow blacks routinely made "bad" choices because they had been made to feel by "civil rights" activists and supporters that society offered them no opportunities. And today these activists -- many of whom are white and don't have to pay the price -- continue to circulate the same messages of despair. By exploiting and sensationalizing black failure, the Left has created a mood of dejection among young blacks that must be broken if we are to make real progress in the '90s. For blacks, a better world will not come riding on the coattails of government spending, affirmative action, AFDC, and other government initiatives, but through our own efforts. As Carter G. Woodson wrote in *The Miseducation of the Negro*: "History shows that it does not matter who is in power ... those who have not learned to do for themselves and have to depend on others never obtain any more rights and privileges in the end than they had in the beginning."

5

After Civil Rights

Walter Williams

The modern part of the black civil rights movement started with the *Brown v. Board of Education* case in 1954. Looking back, it was important to end legalized school segregation and discriminatory school financing. After all, education is one of the most important ingredients for upward socioeconomic mobility. It was also important to attack the harmful educational discriminatory policy engineered by whites in their roles as mayors, school superintendents, and principals.

It is now some 36 years later. We have experienced the promise of busing. We have fought valiantly and won positions as mayors in eight out of the twelve major cities and hold key management positions in many others. In many cities, blacks are school superintendents, hold prominent positions on school boards, are school principals, and are widely represented among teachers, counselors, and consultants.

Now the question is: who is prepared to stand up and say that black education today is anything near what those who fought and won the *Brown* struggle in 1954 thought it might have been in 1990? In fact, if anything, black education may be worse. In 1954, I graduated from Benjamin Franklin, Philadelphia's worst high school. Neither I, nor kids who went to school with me, can remember knowing of other kids our age who could not read or fill out a job application form. In 1954, and all before, Philadelphia's mayor was white, its superintendent was white, all school principals were white and only three times, in 12 years of schooling, did I have a black teacher. Today, in Philadelphia, the mayor, the school superintendent, principals, and most teachers are black. With blacks running schools, black education is worse than when whites were running them.

I am not here to assess blame. My modest agenda is to try to get people to change the way we think about the problems black people face today. I am trying to get people who really care to consider that the problems black people face today are, for the most part, not civil rights problems. As I see it, the civil rights struggle is essentially over and won. Blacks have the same constitutional protections as whites. If we continue to think of black educational problems as a civil rights issue, we will continue with policies like busing and integration, trying to get more money for public schools, college affirmative action programs for young blacks who cannot meet traditional academic entry requirements and banning employment tests. Seeing black miseducation as something cooked up by white racists will allow us to ignore the self-induced day-to-day destruction of our youngsters at the primary and secondary levels, in the home and in the neighborhoods. Allow me to be a bit more specific by listing activities not conducive to acquiring a good education, which are often routine in predominantly black schools and homes. There is widespread assault, which includes rape and murder; gross property destruction; high rates of absenteeism and dropout; many incompetent and poorly motivated teachers; poor learning attitudes and lack of school reinforcement in the home.

These activities are educationally devastating; yet none of them can be ameliorated by civil rights strategy. Moreover, as long as we assume that the major blame for the tragic state of black education is the lack of civil rights, we can expect this tragic status quo to continue.

My discussion has focused on education just for concreteness, but similar thinking applies to other major problems that black people face. Crime takes a devastating toll in black neighborhoods and blacks are both the victims and the perpetrators. The human cost, borne by those who are raped, mugged, assaulted, burglarized, and murdered, is tragic in and of itself. But there are other costs. The high crime rate makes black neighborhoods inhospitable places to conduct business. Black businessmen find that getting loans and insurance is a costly, if not impossible, proposition. Fewer business opportunities mean fewer local employment opportunities. On top of that, black people must bear the cost of traveling long distances to do routine shopping chores. Crime also means that anything in black neighborhoods is of lower value. Consider the fact that houses in black neighborhoods that could not fetch $30,000 all of a sudden become worth $100,000 and $200,000 when they are renovated and gentrified (whites move in).

Again, if we view crime as caused by poverty and discrimination, a civil rights problem, poor blacks are doomed to the status quo in perpetuity. It is like saying that a few blacks shall be allowed to terrorize the many until white people decide to act right. I am always struck by those who put the crime problem in black neighborhoods at the doorstep of racism and poverty. Such an explanation cannot explain why black neighborhoods were far more civil and economically robust, in the '30s, '40s, and '50s at a time when blacks were much poorer and before we had basic civil rights. Such an observation should tell us that racism and poverty cannot be the full explanation for what we see today. If so, why was it not worse yesterday?

The civil rights struggle has yielded great fruits for most blacks who find their lives the envy of their grandparents. But for a large, and increasing, number of blacks upward mobility remains elusive, even though they have civil rights. They have been made, or have become, immune to the traditional routes out of poverty and the effects of a robust economy, such as that experienced over the last seven years, and educational opportunity. They will remain so as long as we continue to view the problem as one of civil rights.

6

The Movement Continues

Juan Williams

I'm struck by the suggestion that somehow the civil rights movement is over, that we can even talk about "after civil rights." I can tell you, as someone who goes often onto college campuses, that people who are seniors in the college world today, born in '68 or after, have never been involved with the civil rights movement, and never fought in it.

In fact, what you see is an overwhelming romanticism about the '60s among these generations. It's a romanticism that begins with the thought: "Oh, my God, if King were alive, then we would know what to do. Then the movement would be going forward." Or something like it, which says: "Well, the '60s was when it was happening. If this were the '60s, I'd be involved. I'd be doing something. Malcolm was right. Riots were right. Violence was right. That's when things were really moving. That's when change was possible in American society." And they equate the idea of protest and marches with the idea of true change in American society.

Well, my attitude towards this nostalgia is that the civil rights movement in fact never ended. It ended only if you think of it simply in terms of a first assault on the barriers of segregation, in terms of the Civil Rights Act, the Voting Rights Act, or an attempt at a Fair Housing Act. But the reality to my mind is that this movement is really much broader than simply some government program aimed at ending segregation -- that, really, when we talk about the movement, we talk about the original sin of this society, the deprivation of rights visited upon people on the basis of the color of their skin. We talk about slavery. We talk about segregation. And we talk about the repercussions that that history has for us even to this day.

So that when we talk about the current incarnation of the civil rights movement, to my mind, we are talking about economics, we are talking about the social reality which is, you know, so difficult to ignore as we watch poverty advance to engulf the lives of more and more of our children.

We talk about the reality of half of all black children being born in poverty today.

We talk about the reality of income disparities continuing even for people of equal education in this society, continuing on the basis of race.

We talk about the lack of economic opportunity and what it has done to this generation of black people.

In short, it seems to me that we are in fact talking about the *continuation* of a historic moment, the civil rights movement is not something that can be bracketed and said to be over. It is a central theme of America's history.

But just as I say this, I've got to say that there has been a tremendous corruption of the concept of political movement -- or civil rights movement -- within the last decade or so, and that much of this corruption unfortunately has come from the civil rights side of the aisle. Over the last 10 years, maybe even 20, it seems to me that the idea of getting over, or getting yours, has become far too prevalent a motif among black political leaders. I am referring to the idea that seems to be endemic now that blacks have their part of the pie and that every company, every unit of government, should simply have their one part, their vice president in charge of personnel who deals with blacks, their black music division. This is true now all over. Corporate America can somehow buy peace with the black community and typically do so by buying some civil rights figure to stand up and speak for them. And this is how the civil rights groups tend to get money and tend to get by -- because they fuel this guilt trip attitude, fuel the idea that somehow blacks can be bought and that the civil rights movement is for sale.

Similarly, black political power has been corrupted. In Newark, Ken Gibson was reelected under indictment -- in the name of somehow "we got to stick with the brother." The idea is that black politicians have not had a chance before, and no matter how far down they take you, they need to be supported. You look at a city like Gary, Indiana, and Hatcher, and again you see sort of the negative side of black political power. You look at what's going on in my hometown here, Washington, D.C., with the indictment of Marion Barry, and again you see the dark side of this phenomenon -- in which the Movement gets distorted. The Movement is used to defend politicians who by all measure should absolutely be hooted out of office.

But again, while I regret to see this kind of development because it undermines our power -- it takes away the moral righteousness of the movement -- it must be said that what has really fueled this attitude over the last 10 years has been Ronald Reagan. It has been the Right, because the Right over the last 10 years, it seems to me, has once again engaged in racial politics.

It seems to me that Mr. Reagan has been sending out a drum beat from this town that says, "Well, you know, we've done enough on this civil rights stuff. We don't need to do any more." We don't need to disrupt our lives by talking about busing, by talking about affirmative action. Instead, let us distort Martin Luther King's message and talk about the ideal of a color blind society. Ask everyone involved to be absolutely ahistorical -- in more simplistic terms, to be dumb and ignorant and to ignore the history of this country and somehow pretend that we can all start at the same place and achieve the same thing.

Well, it seems to me that once you go down this road, once you begin to practice this kind of racial politics, then you will see the careers of Jesse Jackson and Al Sharpton, Louis Farrakhan, even David Duke, take off with new vigor because they are able to feed on the animosity.

Once you get into this kind of situation, both sides begin sniping at the other. You get into a situation where you have young white people forming groups like the National Association for the Advancement of White People, which they have at Penn State -- as if whites had somehow been the oppressed for the majority of history of this country. You free this monster of alienation and antagonism at just the moment when in our society we have heightened competition for spots in schools, jobs, promotions, and people soon get the idea that somehow you can point fingers at other people. You can absolutely demean other people by saying they have had bad values, criminal behaviors, bad schools, engage in welfare scams; in short, it's the problem of the black community, and, well, blacks really aren't up to the fight. They clearly can't compete at the same level, and, therefore, don't worry about it. We'll give them theirs and go on our merry way.

In the face of these facts and considering all these realities, it seems to me that we're at a new phase of the civil rights movement, that this movement has clearly not ended. It seems to me that there's a more compelling need than ever for people to become activated, to think about how to address civil rights issues in the '90s.

It seems to me very clear that as historians look back on the '90s, the question they ask will not be whether the movement ended. It will be what incarnation the movement was taking during this period. And to my mind, people will be talking about the economic split, the polarization along economic lines as much as along racial lines, that is now current in American society.

They'll be talking about the new resegregation taking place -- most evident in our schools, big city schools which are now overwhelmingly composed of blacks and typically offer inferior quality education, not allowing people to become full human beings.

When historians look back at this period, this will be the reality of 1990, and in that context, the question of whether or not the movement is over seems to me to be a rhetorical fantasy, and one that we can't really afford at this moment.

7

Race: The Issue

Joe Klein

On a pleasant spring evening, several weeks before New York was convulsed by the rape of the woman jogger in Central Park, Richard Ravitch found himself in the heart of Queens -- pressing his long-shot candidacy for mayor -- trying to sell optimism to a room full of pessimists. "This city was built by optimists," he insisted. "By people who built the subways two stops beyond where the newest houses were going up. By people who built reservoirs, and roads, and bridges, an infrastructure far more sophisticated and expensive than was needed -- because they had faith in the idea of New York, they knew the city would grow and prosper...."

"It was different then," the man next to me muttered. This was an audience of mutterers -- the Continental Regular Democratic Club: elderly Jews mostly, the sort of people who sit behind you in matinees and repeat the dialogue.

Ravitch plodded ahead, sensing that his attempt at urban rhapsody wasn't quite cutting it with this crowd, but pushing on anyway -- to the immigrant experience, usually a winner with older folks. They loved to hear about the "wave after wave" of immigrants who came to New York "with a dream of building a life for themselves and their families. This city is an incubator," he said. "It provides an atmosphere of opportunity for each newly arrived group, where they can get a job, an education for their children, and move into the mainstream..."

"So what happened?" An elderly woman interrupted. "What about the --"

Race: The Issue originally appeared in **New York Magazine**, 29 May 1989.

"Shhhh," said the man in front of her.

"No, let me say it," she said, putting a hand on the man's shoulder.

"Get your hand off me!" he yelled, and moved away. "Let him talk."

These were wild, inexplicable passions. Ravitch seemed lost, deflated: What was going on here? "Excuse me, Mr. Ravitch," said Arthur Katzman, a leader of the Continental Dems and a longtime member of the City Council. "But I must disagree with you about the immigrants. It was true of the immigrants who came from Europe, and also the Orientals. But these ... others. The quality is not as good. The ability to contribute used to be greater." There was wild applause, which Katzman took to mean that it was time for a speech -- and he careened off on a defense of the mayor and a tour of the homeless crisis, thereby relieving the candidate of the need to respond to that other question.

In a perfect world, Ravitch -- whose lifelong devotion to the cause of civil rights is unimpeachable -- would have gone back and chastised Katzman for the racial implication of his comments. He might have mentioned the thousands of West Indians and Hispanics who have opened stores and worked their way into the mainstream, the tens of thousands of American blacks who -- against all odds -- have gone to college, become teachers and nurses and public officials. A truly gutsy response would have gone on to acknowledge the social anarchy that has overtaken the black underclass, and the difficulties the city -- and the nation -- faces in trying to deal with it. But Ravitch should be forgiven his stunned evasion: Each of his fellow candidates would have done the same.

Race is an issue that politicians go to great pains to avoid. It has been deemed unfit for open discussion, in all but the most platitudinous manner, for many years. The public is, oddly, complicit in this: People seem to sense that the topic is so raw, and their feelings so intense, that it's just too risky to discuss in mixed company. "It never comes up," says another mayoral hopeful. "Crime does all the time, but it's rarely linked to race. I get the questions and comments in public meetings about everything under the sun -- but never about race."

In private, though, race seems the only thing people are talking about these days -- especially since the terrifyingly casual barbarism in Central Park last month. The radio talk shows, the true vox pop of the '80s, are full of it. The subject dominates fancy dinner parties in Manhattan; it comes up on supermarket lines in Queens and around kitchen tables in Brooklyn; it has suddenly become permissible to vent frustrations, to ask questions and say things -- often ugly things -- that have been forbidden in polite discourse for many years.

And the central question, at least among whites, is a version -- more or less refined -- of what Arthur Katzman was trying to get across in Queens that night: Why have so many blacks proved so resistant to incubation? Why, after 25 years of equal rights -- indeed, of special remedial treatment under law -- do so many remain outside the bounds of middle-class society? Why do even educated blacks seem increasingly remote, hostile, and paranoid? In a society besotted with quick fixes and easy answers to every problem, is this the one that will prove insoluble?

Even though none of the candidates will say it publicly, race is the central issue in this year's mayoral campaign. But then, it was the great unspoken in last year's presidential election as well -- remember Willie Horton? It is, and always has been, the most persistent and emotional test of America's ability to exist as a society of equals. In New York, the challenge is immediate and explosive: Race is at the heart of all of the city's most critical problems -- crime; drugs; homelessness; the crises in public education, public health, and children's services. All have been exacerbated by racial polarization and antagonism. And also by a conspiracy of silence -- by a fear of speaking candidly about the causes and possible solutions to these problems.

The silence may well be about to end. Each new outrage -- Howard Beach, Tawana Brawley, the constant drumbeat of crack killings, cops blown away, the jogger raped, the black woman raped and thrown off the Brooklyn rooftop (one of the legion of black victims ignored by white society) -- each new barbarity nudges people closer to the moment when the discussion of how black and white Americans can come to terms with each other is reopened.

It is a public debate that was closed down abruptly nearly 20 years ago. The country has been drifting toward disaster ever since. "There is an illness in the community now, a psychosis," says John Lewis, the Georgia congressman and one of the true heroes of the civil-rights movement. "We need to bring all the dirt and all the sickness out into the open. We need to talk again about building what Dr. King called a beloved community -- a truly integrated society of blacks and whites."

Integration seems an impossible romantic notion now. Even to propose it as the solution to the racial morass raises derisive hoots in the black community and patronizing shrugs and smiles from whites. Serious talk of integration ended when "black power" began to flourish and equal rights were supplanted by affirmative action as the rallying cry of the movement. Aggrievement -- the notion that blacks deserved special community compensatory treatment -- replaced assimilation at the top of the activists' agenda. Integration withered as a goal; "community control" replaced it. The movement imploded -- and white America was only too happy to let it happen. Liberals quickly, romantically -- and quite irresponsibly -- acceded to the new black demands; conservatives were quietly relieved that blacks no longer wanted in. Only a few brave souls raised the obvious question: How could blacks be included in American society if they insisted on separating themselves from it? For the most part, interracial debate ended.

"White America ceded control of the definition of the problem to blacks in the late '60s and early '70s," says Glenn Loury, a black professor of political economy at Harvard's Kennedy School. "But not control of the solution. A situation of mutually reinforcing cowardice has resulted."

Twenty years later, having suffered a generation of black "power" and white indifference, race relations are at a dead end. The usual litany of achievement -- the growth of a black middle class, the integration of public life -- isn't very convincing. The horrific desperation of the black underclass demands that the racial debate be reopened, and the only logical place for it to begin is where it left off: at the moment when the civil rights movement resegregated itself. "We made a serious mistake when the movement turned against its first principle: integration," John Lewis laments. "The seeds that were planted 20 years ago have borne very bitter fruit."

The shift from integration to "black power" seems a strange, counterproductive inversion now -- and yet it seemed perfectly logical at the time. How did it happen -- and happen so quickly? The death of Martin Luther King Jr. is often cited as a turning point -- Lewis mentions it -- but Stokely Carmichael proclaimed "black power" two years before King's death, and Malcolm X was drawing large crowds well before that. The separatist impulse had always been there, ever since emancipation -- and so its revival in the mid-'60s was no great surprise. The surprise was the speed with which it moved from a handful of radicals at the periphery to the heart of the civil rights movement. The irony was that it occurred at a moment when civil rights legislation -- bills that mandated integration -- were flying through Congress and the leading integrationist, Martin Luther King, was winning the Nobel Peace Prize. Never had America seemed so open to the idea of inclusion.

And yet the legislation -- particularly the Voting Rights Act of 1965 -- contained the seeds of separatism. As Bayard Rustin, a stalwart integrationist until his death in 1987, pointed out early on, "What began as a protest movement is now being challenged to translate itself into a political movement." This meant a shift from nonviolent demonstrations to "the building of community institutions or power bases" to elect black politicians.

There wasn't much percentage in integration for the black mayors and aldermen who soon won election across the black belt in the South and in the urban slums up North. For people like Charles Evers, running for mayor of Fayette, Mississippi, black electoral power was a far more immediate concern than the gauzy ideal of "black-and-white together." Their agenda was naturally compensatory: If the streets on the white side of town were paved, equality meant paving them on the black side of town. Like all good politicians, the new black officials pandered to their core constituencies. This was classic ethnic politics, a healthy impulse -- but it put the black pols into closer rhetorical proximity with the militant separatists: Both were calling for "black power."

Northern black leaders wanted a piece of the action, too -- but they were locked into larger, white-dominated government entities. For them, the naked choice was between power and integration: By separating from the white system -- by demanding "community control" of school districts in New York, for example -- they could gain a measure of power from the white politicians who ran the town. As Nicholas Lemann observed in *The Atlantic* last December and January, the "community action" component of the federal war on poverty reinforced this tendency by funneling money to a new generation of community leaders, instead of to the established city authorities -- even Lyndon Johnson, it seemed, believed in black power.

There was, less obviously, a certain security in separatism as well. If the schools (and neighborhoods) remained black, there was a good chance blacks would run them. Integration challenged blacks as profoundly as it did whites. It meant competing against *the man* for the top jobs. And a great many blacks were convinced -- despite all the new laws and King's Nobel Prize and a president who said, "We shall overcome" -- that the competition would be as unfair as it always had been. There were, quite understandably, more than a few who quietly wondered if the racists were right, and secretly feared that they couldn't compete. "That impulse was nothing new," said a labor leader deeply involved in the civil rights movement. "The black teachers in the South were pretty solidly against integration in the 1950s."

So the militants provided the new black class of political leaders with a philosophical rationale for their natural impulses to accumulate power and avoid competition: White society was fundamentally racist, and so integration was pointless. Blacks were victims of a systematic oppression and deserved special treatment -- affirmative action, quotas, more programs of every sort -- in recompense. This was quite satisfying intellectually. Many fair-minded Americans agreed: Blacks had been treated abominably. Their restraint in the face of the most noxious provocation had been remarkable. Even when the great urban riots began in the mid-'60s, these seemed an understandable -- if not justifiable -- response to white prejudice.

But a line was crossed when blacks demanded -- and then got -- special treatment. A price was paid, most immediately in heightened antagonism from the white working class, which felt threatened by the new rules. But eventually by the blacks themselves: By defining themselves as victims and separating themselves by race, they had guaranteed their continued isolation from white society. "This ... is the tragedy of black power in America today," wrote Shelby Steele, the brillant black essayist, in *Harper's* last year. "It is primarily a victim's power ... Whatever gains this power brings in the short run through political action, it undermines in the long run. Social victims may be collectively entitled, but they are all too often individually demoralized."

When aggrievement was proclaimed the central, psychic fact of life, the most aggrieved and alienated -- the most amoral, the criminals -- became the definers of "true" blackness in the media and also in the streets. White liberals, guilt-ridden (I write from experience), accepted this spurious definition at face value. Far worse, though: For a brief, truly revolting moment, white radicals celebrated the most antisocial blacks as culture heroes. Criminality was romanticized. Slums were now called "ghettos," which assumed a romantic communalism and immediacy of oppression that simply didn't exist.

The radical looniness reached its apex with the celebration of the Black Panthers and of Eldridge Cleaver's hopelessly perverted *Soul on Ice*, in which black-on-white rape was described as a political act. (As a young reporter in Boston at the time, I interviewed a white rape victim who coolly described her post-violation reaction: "I went to the free clinic to get a tetanus shot, and then went home and reread Eldridge Cleaver, so I could better understand what happened.") There was something incredibly careless -- so ironic as to feed the worst black paranoia -- about both the white radicals' celebration and the liberals' acceptance of this pathological behavior. By romanticizing these irresponsible activities -- criminality, sexual "freedom," drug use, and general lack of ambition -- whites were lending support to a subtle system of oppression that had existed since slavery times.

"One can think of the lower-class Negroes as bribed and drugged by this system," wrote John Dollard in his landmark 1937 study *Caste and Class in a Southern Town*. "The effect of the social set-up seems to be to keep Negroes infantile, to grant them infantile types of freedom from responsibility.... The evidence is unmistakable that the moral indolence allowed to Negroes is perceived by them and their white caste masters as a compensating value and gain [for forced labor in a plantation or share-cropping system]."

The words seem rather harsh now, after a quarter-century of euphemisms. But John Dollard wrote as a firm advocate of "Negro" rights; he described a pattern of oppression and prescribed a solution. He made a clear distinction between the determinedly proper black middle class, struggling to assimilate, and the rural underclass, which had not yet shed the behavior patterns imposed by their former slave masters. Then he concluded, "The dominant aim of our society seems to be to middle-classify all of its members. Negroes, including lower-class Negroes, are not exceptions. Eventually they must all enter the competition for higher status which is so basic and compulsive an element in our way of life. This will mean ... approximating more nearly the ideal of restraint, independence and personal maturity competition and mobility."

This was considered radical race-mixing in the '30s; thirty years later, black activists had come to see any derogation of lower-class black morality as white paternalism. When Daniel Patrick Moynihan wrote a report -- in the spirit of Dollard -- on the instability of black family structure in 1965, he was pilloried. A sociological ice age ensued. "Liberals became increasingly reluctant to research, write about, or publicly discuss inner-city social dislocations following the virulent attacks against Moynihan," wrote the black sociologist William Julius Wilson in *The Truly Disadvantaged*. Indeed, for nearly 20 years, the only "legitimate" research was conducted by "minority scholars on the strengths, not the weaknesses, of inner-city families and communities."

Meanwhile, the pathology metastasized. When Moynihan wrote his report in 1965, a "staggering" 26 percent of non-white children were born out of wedlock; now the figure is 61 percent. The technology of underclass indolence also has exploded: The Saturday-night knife fights on the black side of the tracks that Dollard says the rednecks found so amusing have become shoot-outs with semi-automatic weapons; "white lightning" has become crack. Sex remains sex -- but mixed with hypodermic needles spells AIDS.

A great many blacks and white liberals will argue that these spiraling pathologies are the result of racism, the hopelessness and frustration that are part of growing up desperately poor and "knowing" that the system won't cut you any slack. This is undoubtedly true, as is William Julius Wilson's belief that the departure of the black middle class from the cities to the suburbs removed role models, disciplinarians, and other socializing forces from the slums, hastening the collapse of the social order. "You can't imagine how removed these kids are from life as we know it," says Andrew Cuomo, who runs a program for homeless families. "They have no contact with anyone who has succeeded in the system. They don't have an uncle who's a lawyer or an aunt who's a teacher. They see no point to succeeding. The line you hear most often is 'Stay in school so you can go to work at a McDonald's.'"

This terrible deprivation no doubt would have existed if sociologists had been free to ply their trade in the slums, and if the civil-rights movement had kept integration as its goal, but the militant know-nothingism of the black nationalists certainly hasn't helped any. Sadly, when "black power" filters to the streets, it's often little more than a rationale for failure: More than a few scholarly studies, notably one by John U. Ogbu and Signithia Fordham in *The Urban Review*, have shown that there is enormous peer pressure against academic success in black high schools. It is considered "acting white."

The taunts that Ogbu and Fordham describe seem no worse than those endured by generations of Jewish, Irish, and Italian nerds, but the sanctions are cosmic: The black kid who succeeds in school is not only a traitor to the race but a sucker besides. He, or she, is busting his butt for a job at McDonald's. There is tremendous pressure on these kids -- even those from strict, stable middle-class homes, as some of the children involved in the Central Park rape apparently were -- to prove their blackness by misbehaving.

White society offers very few incentives to the black teenagers who resist peer pressure and play "our" game. Indeed, they are treated with the same disdain visited upon the potential hoodlums. In a stunning bit of television several weeks ago, Ted Koppel gave six star black high-school students a camera and sent them out into the white world, asking for change of a dollar. The reactions were depressing. Most whites simply ignored the kids. White women were startled when approached; one seemed to jump back, then hastened to the other side of the street.

Given the levels of criminality, these reactions are also understandable. They are part of the vicious spiral of racism and reaction that has been allowed to spin out of control during the years of silence. The pattern is clear: The more violent the streets become, the more race-sensitive whites become, and the blacks, in turn, grow more isolated and angry. The rape of the jogger in Central Park seems to have ratcheted the cycle another turn toward anarchy. The white reaction is manifest. Mayoral candidates who never hear questions about race relations in public forum say that privately white people seem obsessed by the incident. "Jaws have tightened," says another -- that is, they have no tolerance for discussions of racism, oppression, or other excuses for antisocial behavior.

The reaction in the black community is less remarked upon but no less extreme and much more disturbing. "I am just disgusted by how many friends tell me that it was the jogger's fault," says one prominent black leader. "They say she shouldn't have been there."

There is also a new outbreak of the half-crazed paranoia and conspiracy-theorizing that have become quite popular in the black media in recent years. *The City Sun*, considered a "respectable" black weekly, published a truly vomitous account of the incident, including a fantasy description of the victim's body as "the American Ideal ... a tiny body with round hips and pert buttocks, soft white thighs, slender calves, firm and high breasts."

The author of this trash went on to opine that -- if you omit the question of whether the rape actually occurred -- the children who committed the Central Park abomination were being subjected to the same sort of treatment as the Scottsboro boys, the blacks falsely convicted of raping a white woman in Alabama 50 years ago. This sort of nonsense is of a piece with the increasing numbers of blacks nationally who, according to one pollster, believe that the drug crisis is a conspiracy on the part of white society to "commit genocide" against blacks. "The really disturbing thing is that the more solid the black middle class becomes," this pollster said, "the more its fundamental views of the issues seems to diverge from middle-class America."

In the days since his untimely death, I have been thinking about the asthma that killed Schools Chancellor Richard Green. I had several long conversations with Green during his year or so as chancellor, and the most striking thing about him -- in addition to his fierce integrity and caring -- was how constricted he seemed, physically and figuratively. This was especially true when we were "on the record." He would speak in word clouds, imprecise, cliched and formal, his inhaler clutched tightly in his hand. When I put the notebook away -- and no longer was an official emissary of the white media -- he literally seemed to breathe easier. We gossiped freely about politicians and reporters, and how strange the flushed intensity of New York seemed to a fellow from the eminently more rational town of Minneapolis.

The pressure of my "official" station on this proud man -- and his relief when the inquisition ended -- is haunting. The Richard Green's of the world, all the striving, insistently moral black men and women working to overcome 400 years of stereotyping, are the most poignant victims of the escalating alienation between the races. They are the tightrope walkers, holding their breath as they perform in midair with only a slender strand of support -- ever fearful that even the smallest mistake will prove cataclysmic.

I wonder what can be done to make their lives easier, to show appreciation for their efforts. The usual impulse -- the liberal impulse -- is to look to government for a remedy, and there are some things that can be done, but a great deal that can't. The most basic thing, I suspect, is to implement John Dollard's 50-year-old prescription: Make a concerted effort to undo the behavior patterns of the underclass that cause social anarchy, feed the cycle of racism, and undercut the efforts of middle-class blacks to become part of the larger society.

For a quarter-century, this agenda has been avoided. There have been two paradigms for dealing with dilemmas of race, and neither has worked. Conservatives have ignored the problem, left the solution to "market forces" or, worse, to social Darwinism. Liberals seem to have abandoned critical thought entirely, allowing militants to dictate their agenda, scorning most efforts to impose sanctions on antisocial behavior by underclass blacks.

A new model is needed, one that returns to the original movement goals of integration and equal rights while addressing the deterioration that has taken place in black family structure and community institutions over the past 20 years. Integration -- that is, assimilation into the middle-class economy -- can be the only possible goal. The society has to "emphasize commonality as a higher value than 'diversity' or pluralism,'" wrote Shelby Steele in *Harper's*. Programs that divide by race, even well-intentioned ones like affirmative action, are too costly in moral terms. They send the wrong message -- of racial division and aggrievement. A more profitable agenda is one that seeks to pull the poorest, regardless of race, into conformity with middle-class standards. Even now, before a real debate has started, some areas of agreement are beginning to emerge:

Education. Head Start pre-school programs have proven to be successful in helping to adjust poor children to the middle-class educational experience; studies have shown that Head Start graduates are less likely to drop out of high school, more likely to do well academically. Everyone from George Bush to Jesse Jackson praises the program -- and yet it is available to only 16 percent of those eligible. Why? Because it isn't cheap. This year, Head Start will cost $1.235 billion. Multiply that by six.

Perhaps the most important job for schools in the present atmosphere is to convince poor kids that there's hope for them, that they are not being merely hustled on to jobs at McDonald's. In truth, many demographers predict a serious labor shortage in the near future -- a serious skilled-labor shortage already exists -- and good jobs most likely will be there if the kids finish school. But programs like the Boston Compact -- in which local companies guarantee work to every Boston public high school graduate -- can reduce the anxiety of poor teenagers and counteract the sneers of the street kids, the ones too cool to compete. Harrison J. Goldin, the city comptroller and a candidate for mayor, has proposed that more attention also be given to dropout prevention in the early elementary grades.

"Attendance in fourth grade is a strong indicator of which kids will stay in school later on," he says. "Instead of putting our dropout-prevention money at the high-school level, we should be spending it in the earlier grades."

Still schools can do only so much. Indeed, they are blamed for a great deal they can't do. I've had several conversations recently with independent observers who've been spending time in the public schools. "They aren't in crisis," says one, who has concentrated on the early elementary grades around town. "I started off thinking we were faced with a disaster, but I was dead wrong. The teachers are great. The kids are alert. The books and equipment aren't any worse than they were when I was in school. The problem is what goes on outside the classroom -- in the streets, in the homes."

Crime. Strict law enforcement may be the ultimate civil rights program: It removes the temptation of the street as a viable alternative to staying in school. More of everything is needed: more cops, more jails, more drug treatment slots -- and a much more serious attempt by the federal government to interdict the flow of drugs into the country. All of which will cost untold billions.

But perhaps the most valuable thing that can be done in this area is to drive home the certainty of punishment in the slums, to make it an immediate reality for the kids tempted to go wrong. The idea of community work gangs; often dismissed by liberals, isn't quite so Draconian as it sounds. If the kids on the street see the small-time corner drug-dealer busted on Monday, tried, convicted, and forced to scrub graffiti off the local elementary school in a prison work gang by Thursday, it may erase some of the glamour from the drug trade. "They should put the miscreants in really demeaning outfits, too -- like pink polka dots," says one formerly liberal Democrat. "Anything that makes lawbreaking seem less macho and more dumb."

Personal responsibility. This is more controversial and also, most likely, the heart of the problem. How should society address the 15-year-old mother? What does she owe the government in return for the welfare check it gives her? A consensus seems to have grown in favor of "workfare," which was included in last year's federal welfare-reform law. But that's not enough: Doesn't the teenage mother owe society something more than simply going to work after her kids have grown? "She owes us being a good mother," says former U.S. Attorney Rudolph Giuliani, now a declared candidate for mayor. "I wouldn't have any trouble with a requirement that these girls attend parenting classes and bring their babies there....We might encourage them not to have more children and teach them to care for the ones they do have."

But then, a lot of attention has been paid to the problems of teenage mothers. Remarkably, the responsibility of the fathers has been largely ignored. And yet, the "impulse freedom" (as John Dollard called it) involved in siring a child out of wedlock and then refusing to support it is the essential pathology of the black underclass. It represents a state of mind, a behavior pattern that is the most enduring legacy of slavery. Last year's welfare-reform legislation stepped up child-support-enforcement procedures. The question now is how far the society is willing to go: Should the mothers be required to give up the names of their mates? If the fathers aren't working, should they be provided with public-works jobs? Should they be the ones scrubbing graffiti off the local elementary school?

There is no question that the problem of the underclass can't be solved unless an ethic of personal responsibility pervades the entire society, from top to bottom. If black teenagers are going to be made responsible for their sexual conduct, taxpayers will have to be willing to spend the money on education and crime-fighting that will channel the children of the underclass toward inclusion in the middle-class economy. To those few remaining self-destructive militants who say, "You're asking us to become white," the answer is readily apparent in the recent tide of Asian immigrants who practice economic integration while maintaining a fierce cultural pride and even, to an extent, segregating themselves in ethnic enclaves.

"When you are behind in a footrace," Martin Luther King, Jr. told college students in 1964, "the only way to get ahead is to run faster than the man in front of you. So when your white roommate says he's tired and goes to sleep, you stay up and burn the midnight oil."

There is not much more that government can do than help the runners to the starting line and make sure the lanes are clear for all contestants. There is no way government can guarantee that blacks will succeed, although many seem to believe that to be the case. "It's the greatest difference between blacks and whites in polling -- the vast majority of blacks believe government can solve anything," says a prominent pollster. "By contrast, the baby-boomers are the ultimate level-playing-field crowd. If you ask them who gets special benefits from the government, they name three groups: big corporations, rich people, and minorities. The good news is that they seem ready to accept anyone who earns what he gets, regardless of race."

Polling data are notoriously sanguine when it comes to problems of race. No doubt, far too many whites won't be ready to "accept anyone ... regardless of race." But what's the alternative? The costs of not competing -- of using racism as an excuse for paralysis -- have become all too clear these past 20 years. No doubt, the contest will be far more difficult for blacks than it has been for any group that has gone before them. No doubt, a great many won't succeed, and a great many more will be as uncertain and anguished in their pride as Richard Green was. The contest won't be fair.

But consider the possible results of the extra testing, the fearsome struggle that will be required of blacks if they are determined, finally, to compete as equals -- even if the race is still stacked against them: Their triumphs will be that much sweeter; their success may prove that much more spectacular than the victories won by the less rigorously tried "Europeans" and Asians who have incubated so well -- and who have no choice now but to cheer on their African brothers and sisters, since the success of the experiment itself may depend on it.

Part II

Identities

Stanley Crouch

Harmeet Dhillon

Glenn Loury

8

ROLE MODELS

Stanley Crouch

Following my mentors, Albert Murray and Ralph Ellison, I have long maintained that the influence of Afro-Americans on our cultural and political life is indelible and ongoing. Just as it is quite easy to see how Negro style has affected our music, our language, our humor, our dance, and even our ways of walking and performing sports, we cannot deny the impact Afro-Americans have had on this country's movement toward the realization of the ideals that cluster in the heart of our democratic conception.

In a long and tragic series of confrontations, black Americans have had to scale, bore through, or detonate the prejudicial walls that blocked access to the banquet of relatively unlimited social advancement that we know is the grand inspirational myth of American life. This epic confrontation with bigoted policies reached its heroic movement, bringing together troops that crossed all racial lines, classes, religions, and political parties.

The civil rights movement entered an arena of political engagement that demanded dousing redneck dragon fire, transforming segregationists like Lyndon Johnson, battling the paranoid illnesses of men like J. Edgar Hoover, and holding at bay all the hysterically cynical tendencies toward self-pity and defeatist sulking or name-calling in our ranks. The result was both a monumental shift in the national perception of racial matters and an unprecedented entree to the processes of democratic life.

What we learned during those years is that the role of American democracy has come to be one of constant expansion, of inclusive motion beyond one group or one sex to all groups in both sexes. And at this point in our history, the democratic idea has grown even to include the ideal that both the animate and inanimate environment should have the right not to be callously exploited.

But for all the expansions of our conception of democracy and for all the victories against discriminatory attitudes and policies over the last 25 years, we still find ourselves facing the job of improvising the best way of going about making the democratic imperatives at the center of our society function with the sort of vitality that inspires comprehensive engagement. From my position on the battlefield, I have come to believe that a large part of what must be addressed is the nature of the enemy within, the influential dimensions of what must finally be recognized as a vision of American society that leads not toward democratic vibrance but the limitations of Balkanization. In fact, I now believe what has too much impact on the discussion of race is a body of ideas that reflect the amount of decay that has taken place in the Afro-American intellectual, political, and lower class communities.

The battle with so-called "white middle class standards" that we still hear discussed when the subjects of everything from school performance to rap records are addressed is itself a distortion of the goals of the Civil Rights Movement. This battle would lead us to believe that there are differences so great in this society that we could actually accept a separatist vision in which the elemental necessity of human identification across racial, sexual, and class lines would be replaced by the idea that people from various backgrounds can only identify with those from their own groups. Such a conception avoids King's idea that people should be judged by the content of their character and not by the color of their skin -- or, if we extend that to include sex, by gender.

The nature of ethnic nationalism and of gender antagonism that has polluted so much contemporary discussion misses the point of the March on Washington in symbolic terms -- that this culture is usually bettered when we have as many people as possible intelligently interacting, when quality takes precedence over point of social origin, class, race, sex, nationality, and religion. Those who came forward in the late '60s and began to trumpet the idea that there were two Americas -- one black, one white -- not only ignored all of the regional complexities of North, South, Midwest, Southwest, and West, but of Catholic and Protestant, Christian and Jew, as well as all of the variations that break down inside such large categories as white, black, Hispanic, Jew, and American Indian. Now those simplifications have enlisted feminism in making the white male the same thing that he is inside the cosmology of the Nation of Islam: the source of all evil.

This simplification is at odds with the realities of human interaction within our society, and it suggests that those removed from the proverbial seats of power are invariably limited in their freedom to be inspired. We can see that quite easily if we look at something like the controversy at Harvard, where the demand has been raised that a tenured black female be hired by the Law School. No one can be disturbed by a first class black female professor being hired by the department, but the argument that has begun to vibrate with hysteria about such matters implies a fundamental inferiority on the part of black female students. If we were to listen to the activists, we would conclude that black females are so incapable of identifying across racial lines that they cannot look at Sandra Day O'Connor on the Supreme Court and feel that there is a place for them in the American legal profession, perhaps one of extraordinary import someday.

Nothing in my own experience or in the experience of Afro-Americans I have met or read about corroborates the idea that, to any significant extent, people of color are only capable of being inspired by their own race or sex. To suggest that is to distort the heroic engagement that defines Negro history, a good measure of which has always been about struggling with any exclusive conception of human possibility or human identification. Yet we are now supposed to accept the idea that if a black child is looking at Kenneth Branaugh's remarkable film of Shakespeare's *Henry V*, that he or she will not be intrigued by the insights into the problems of power and struggle, of class and cultural clash, but will only be bored or feel left out because the work is something written by "a dead white man about dead white people." In its very provincialism and its racist conception of culture, such an idea opposes the richness of the best of Afro-American culture, regardless of class.

It is due to the distortions of people such as James Baldwin that we have come to believe in far too many instances that black people are such victims of racism that they are as limited as the most provincial superstitions of discrimination that society has believed in for far too many years. Having been born December 14, 1945, in Los Angeles, California, I can say that the people in my community, which was not so much blue collar as blues collar, were forever encouraging all of us to aspire to the very best that we could achieve and were always at war with any idea that would result in our accepting the ethnic limits encouraged by the traditions of segregated thought. Though my mother was a domestic worker who earned sometimes no more than $11 a day and often worked six days a week, she was always cutting out editorials for me to read, bringing home books that her employers either gave her or loaned, and wasn't above forcing me against my will to watch Laurence Olivier's *Richard III* when it came on, or doing the same thing when Orson Welles's *Macbeth* was shown nightly on the "The Million Dollar Movie," which I had to keep looking at until I came to understand what they were saying.

My blues collar mother wasn't being pretentious or exhibiting the effects of having been brain-washed by a "Eurocentric" conception of cultural values. I was never given the impression that I was looking at some great white people strutting some great white stuff. That wasn't the idea at all. My mother knew that Olivier was a great actor and that Shakespeare was a great dramatist. She wanted me to know and experience those facts. She also told me about Marian Anderson, Duke Ellington, Jackie Robinson, and anybody else who represented exemplary achievement. The same was true in public school, where we read Julius Caesar aloud in class, saw films about Marian Anderson and Jackie Robinson, read Dickens and so on. We were constantly taught that great significance is not the franchise of any single group and that we were supposed to identify with the best from whomever and wherever in the world it happened to come. We were not allowed to give any excuses for poor performance either. If we had come up with some so-called "cultural difference" excuse, we would have been laughed at, if not whacked on the boody for disrespecting the intelligence of the teacher. Our teachers were tough and supportive. They knew well that the best way to respect so-called minority students was to demand the most of them.

It is not that the adults of my childhood were naive about racial matters. They knew that excellence and bulldog tenacity were the best weapons against the dragons of this society. That was the point of telling us about the struggles of the Andersons and the Robinsons. But the worst thing that you could be within that community at that time was a racist, no matter how obvious the social limitations were. Adults would say to you, "Boy, the lowest thing you can be is a man who spends all his time hating somebody he doesn't even know. You know, if you want to hold a man down in a hole full of mud, you got to get down there in that mud with him, which will make you just as dirty as the man you say you don't like because he's filthy." Those Negroes

I grew up under were always quick to tell you that there were just two kinds of people in the world: those who tried their best to be good and those who didn't care about being bad. They were true democrats, perhaps because they had learned the hard way what it meant when you submitted to the superstition of discrimination. Those adults were just as proud of Branch Rickey as they were of Jackie Robinson, for each symbolized the will and the discipline necessary to expand the idea of democracy into the arena of practice.

The Afro-American tradition of which I speak is a continuation of what we learn from the life of Frederick Douglass, whose career makes it possible to see that all Americans, regardless of point of social origin, are capable of producing those who will do remarkable things. As Albert Murray points out in *The Omni-Americans*, a book all should read who really wish to know something about this country, the embodiment of the 19th century self-made man is Douglass. Even Lincoln knew that. After Lincoln met with Douglass, the Great Emancipator told his secretary that, given Douglass's beginnings as a slave and his present achievements, he was probably "the most meritorious man in the United States." Murray also observes that Harriet Tubman is easily the best example of the pioneer woman, what my grandmother meant when she complimented someone on having "shit, grit, and mother wit." Yet neither of them can be reduced to mere racial heroes. They are symbols of great American achievement against extraordinary odds.

When we address the richness of our heritage, we will understand that national heritage in the context of Western civilization to the degree that we will understand it for what it is -- an astonishing gathering of information from the entire world, a gathering that had its impact at least partially because of the fight against provincialism that fresh information from other cultures demanded. The experiment that is American democracy is an extension of the ideas of the Magna Carta and Enlightenment and is also a social development of the motion away from the idea of a chosen people that arrived in the New Testament. That is why a reduction of the meaning of Western Civilization to "the story of dead white men" and racist exploitation distorts the realities of the ongoing debate that has lifted our social vision beyond the provincial, whether that lifting meant the debate over slavery or women's suffrage or anything else that has hobbled this country's freedom to benefit from its human resources.

The kind of defeatism, paranoia, and alienation that is fomented by the "dead white men" version of Western and national history is dangerous because it is so far from the facts of what those who made so many of the achievements thought of themselves. I have a feeling that Issac Newton and Galileo didn't spend too much time thinking about their skin color. It is hard for me to believe that Newton got up in the morning saying, "Well, here I am, white Isaac Newton in England and, as white Isaac Newton, I think I'll go over here and try to figure out something white about gravity." I also doubt that Galileo said to himself, "Well, as white Galileo, let me look out here as a white man and see how far I can see with my white eyes. I can't see far enough so I guess I'll have to work on a white tool so I can have a white view of the cosmos." Or can one imagine Beethoven battling to get those string quartets right and thinking, "My job as a white man who will some day be dead is to write some white notes and provide the future with the work of a great white dead man." The work of those men was too hard to be limited by such concerns. The history of Negro and women aviators in the history of flying between the invention of the airplane and World War II proves that there were always those who could see past color and gender to the quality of the contribution and what that contribution might offer them in their own lives. And it is that sort of history that we must perpetually reiterate if we have any serious intention of combatting Balkanization.

It is also easy to see that those who have promoted a reductive vision of Afro-American identity by posturing an antagonistic attitude toward "white middle class standards" would do well to think about the differences between those students who come out of the Business School at Florida A&M University and those students whom anthropologists Signithia Fordham of Rutgers University and John U. Ogbu of Berkeley studied at Capital High School in Washington, D.C. At the predominantly black Florida A&M, Sybil C. Mobley, dean and creator of the Business School, has developed a program over the last 16 years that is recognized by Hewlett-Packard recruiters as one of the top five in the country that produce first level students of finance. In the April 18, 1990, *New York Times* article about the program, it is observed that Mobley forged a curriculum that places as much emphasis on deportment, verbal skills, dress, grooming, and writing abilities as on the details of business. According to the article, Mobley's two-tiered curriculum is "one that some major American companies say the top business schools would do well to emulate." Given the high degree of interest in its business students, Florida A&M has shown that the best thing for so-called minority students is to demand that they engage the specifics of the world in which they live, not to retreat into visions of victimization that diminish the will and thwart the discipline necessary to make one's own way in our society. As one of the female students says of what Mobley has built, "I know who I am. If you know who you are, you don't have to run around in a dashiki. There's a time to do that and a time to wear a suit." Eurocentric? Hardly. That is actually a reiteration of the Afro-American tradition of seeking to be the best within the terms of one's chosen arena.

Just one week later in the *Times,* the disturbing observations of the study of those high school students in Washington, D.C. were reported. The fundamental findings of Fordham and Ogbu give us important insights into some of the elements that explain what has become a noticeable performance gap between white and black students on Scholastic Aptitude Tests and in college work. Though neither the SAT scores nor college performances are discussed in the article, the idea that black students have about what constitutes ethnic authenticity says much about substandard academic achievement by Negroes. Such a circumscribed conception of "blackness" now so influences young black people that, according to the study of those high school students, "They chose to avoid adopting attitudes and putting in enough time and effort in their schoolwork because their peers (and they themselves) would interpret their behavior as 'white.'" It went on to say that there were more than a "dozen other types of behavior that the students considered 'acting white' -- including "speaking standard English, listening to so-called white music, going to the opera or ballet, studying in the library, going to the Smithsonian Institution, doing volunteer work, camping or hiking, putting on airs and being on time." In other words, anything short of the most provincial way of addressing and assessing the varieties of expression and the possibilities that education exists to illuminate meant rejecting one's ethnic identity. Such self-assured provincialism is, at best, self destructive, and is a tendency that must be fought relentlessly.

It is more than odd that we should find ourselves as Americans faced with these bizarre ideas and their effects not only on the black lower class but, as Jeff Howard and Ray Hammond pointed out in the 1985 *New Republic* article "Rumors of Inferiority," on the Negro middle class as well. What we are seeing is a retreat from community expectations and personal demands of high quality in intellectual areas. As Howard and Hammond point out, "Black leaders too often have tried to explain away these problems by blaming racism or cultural bias in the tests themselves. These factors haven't disappeared. But for many middle-class black Americans who have had access to educational and economic opportunities for nearly 20 years, the traditional protestations of cultural deprivation and educational disadvantage ring hollow." That hollowness and those cliches are surely the result of the Balkanized sense of reality that remains at odds with the best of the Afro-American tradition.

We have some very good examples, however, of what can happen when a so-called minority doesn't find itself burdened with a separatist ideology, when they choose -- as black people once knew they should -- to work at more than complaining and trying to subvert the standards that promote excellence. Asian students have shown that they are capable of confounding their fellow students by rising to the challenges of higher education so consistently and so well that they seem not to understand what too many others consider the most important aspects of the college experience. They don't know that when you go to college you're supposed to pledge a fraternity or sorority, go to a beer bust, sleep through your classes, fail to do your papers, and devote large amounts of time to the problem of becoming popular. They have a misunderstanding. They think they're supposed to study. That's why they call the campus library at Berkeley "Chinatown;" when the library opens, Asian students flood in; when the library closes, Asian students are told to leave. Yet there are those who continue to wonder at the high percentage of Asian students who do so well academically! Deduction is obviously not one of their stronger suits.

The defeatist undertow that so misshapes the thinking of black youth regarding intellectual and career engagement is about more than the lack of "role models" which is usually the explanation. In a letter to Ann Landers published February 25, 1990, in *The Washington Post*, a black middle class reader complained, "Black children need role models. We read and hear too much about black pimps and drug dealers and not enough about blacks who have made it. Maybe this is what happens when the press, radio, and TV are predominantly white." Landers responded, quite rightly, that "the problems facing black youths are the same ones white youths have -- no core family unit, no parental guidance, inadequate education, and joblessness." She went on to write, again, quite correctly, "You lose me when you complain of bias in the field of communications and an absence of black role models. A few who come to mind are Oprah Winfrey, Bill Cosby, Lena Horne, Sidney Poitier, Michael Jordan, Magic Johnson, Walter Payton, Mike Singletary, publishing tycoon John Johnson, Supreme Court Justice Thurgood Marshall, General Colin Powell, attorney Marian Wright Edelman, and Dr. Louis Sullivan of Health and Human Services. I could go on, but I'm sure you get the idea."

What we must question is the nature of the voices that black youth choose to listen to when the difficulties facing our society are under discussion. We must look at the problems that exist as much in the black media as in the general media. It is incredible that neither of the two largest black papers in New York -- *The Amsterdam News* and *The City Sun* -- has ever done its job in terms of assessing the scandal of the Tawana Brawley farce and the disreputable roles played by Al Sharpton, Vernon Mason, and Alton Maddox. Nor can we ignore the national trend in black radio to promote paranoid conspiracy theories and to submit to the kind of rabble rousing that avoids the complexity of the various levels of opposition and the necessity of equally complex forms of combat. Nor can we ignore the way in which too many irresponsible intellectuals -- black and white -- have submitted to the youth culture and the adolescent rebellion of pop music, bootlegging liberal arts rhetoric to defend Afro-fascist rap groups like *Public Enemy* on the one hand, while paternalistically defining the "gangster rap" of doggerel chanters such as *Ice Cube* as expressive of the "real" black community. The problem with these tendencies is the same problem that existed when racist iconography dominated media and folklore: semi-literates and illiterates quite often fail to see those things as distortions; they believe they are real. Therefore, it should come as no shock to us when black young people, the products of an oral culture that is ever vulnerable to the dominant voice, sink down into reductive ideas about what they can achieve in this culture.

What must be done is rather obvious. The values of civilized behaviour must be reestablished and defined racially. No one in this society should be allowed to believe that excellence, mastery of our national language, tasteful dress, reliability, or any of the virtues that bring vitality to a society are the sole province of the white population. Welfare laws should be changed so that irresponsible sexual behavior is discouraged by laying the burden of support on the teenage parents, making it in their interest to use birth control

-- if, in fact, they have sex at all. That is not as wild as it immediately sounds. If, for instance, there was a cutoff point -- say, January 1, 1994 -- when it would become law that each teenage parent would be responsible for 45 percent of the support of his or her child and receive only 10 percent of that from welfare agencies, and, that if either parent refused, he or she would be incarcerated in a work-study program from which the monies paid would go to the child's support, the problem would diminish quite rapidly. Those who think that absurd have no understanding of human nature. As an example, let us look at racial attacks in the South from the end of Reconstruction in 1877 until the middle of the 1960s. They were so frequent one would have been led to believe that white men were genetically predisposed to assault black males. Yet those attacks, what journalist Jack Germond recalls as a tradition known as "nigger knocking," fell with true deliberate speed when those who committed such crimes were punished. If something that had gone on for 90 years could be largely reined in when the society refused to allow it, even think of it as normal behavior, are we to believe the problem of teenage pregnancy would sustain itself once young black kids saw it opposed to their self-interest?

At the same time, it is important to note that in a black youth film like *House Party*, Warrington and Reginal Hudlin did something very important: they made it quite clear that the hoodlum element which is so often celebrated in rap recordings is a bane on the black community, something the vast majority of young black people know already. That vision must be reinforced constantly, as it was on *Hill Street Blues*, which never failed to show the costs of crime in so-called minority communities. Those kinds of decisions in mass media are very important because they counter the irresponsiblity of those aforementioned intellectuals who champion or attempt to be sympathetic to anything that shocks or shows contempt for the supposed "white middle class standards" Sybil C. Mobley is so successfully passing on to the students in the Florida A&M Business School.

The Mobleys of this nation should be celebrated and nationally recognized, for they are doing the real work. The public schools of this nation should follow her example and they should get whatever monies are necessary to make them the extraordinary important aspect of democratic success that they once were. We cannot allow our public schools to remain in such bad shape and then wonder why we are having so many social problems. First class teachers, dressing codes, and the reiteration of the importance of the inner life that comes from intellectual development are fundamental to what we must have if this society is to move in the direction of its greatest potential.

We should also think about fresh ways of recognizing Afro-American authenticity. When those who have triumphed and who represent some of the best the country has to offer are discussed, their ethnic identity is often called into question. But when they are jerks, vulgarians, opportunists, and criminals, race is somehow always important. It is time to have the term "black criminal" reversed so that the defining aspect is the criminality, not the race. After all, during the Wall Street scandal the media didn't say "crooked Jewish stockbroker Ivan Boesky," or "another group of Jewish stockbrokers was accused of insider trading." Even John Gotti isn't described as "purported Italian mafia boss." Of course, part of the problem is that manipulators of racial paranoia such as Al Sharpton, Vernon Mason, Alton Maddox, and Marion Barry will inevitably introduce color as an escape hatch. But they must not be allowed to get away with it. The recent elections in Washington, D.C. prove that those who were so willing to support Barry before the cameras didn't at all express the real feelings of the city. The people didn't go for the color con, Lincoln was right: you can't fool all of the people all of the time.

Examples such as Mobley, such as Washington, D.C.'s Kimi Gray, such as the list of achievers that Ann Landers presented, and the country's willingness to embrace virtue and heroic engagement from every quarter of this nation on a scale that has no precedent, make me quite optimistic. We must get back to the grandest vision of this society, which is that all exemplary human endeavor is the heritage of every person. It is the combination of one's ethnic and human heritage that is the issue. Every ethnic group has a heritage of its own and is also heir to symbols of inspiration as different as Magic Johnson and William Shakespeare. All people are heir to everything of wonder that anyone has produced, regardless of race, gender, and place. Anyone who would deny any person identification with the vastness of that marvelously rich offering of human achievement is not truly speaking as an American.

9

Cultural Diversity

Harmeet Dhillon

I was born in India in 1968, in the northern state of Punjab. My parents decided to leave their homeland and come to America for a couple of reasons. As members of a religious minority, the Sikhs, they felt that in a nation such as India, dominated by other religions, their success and happiness would always be circumscribed by their spiritual beliefs, whereas in the United States we would be free to practice our religion without fear of persecution. Moreover, the prospects for education, material success, and personal fulfillment were greater in our new homeland. My father was always fond of reminding us that there were no excuses for not succeeding in America, because in this country people were judged not by the color of their skin or by who their father was, but by their capabilities and achievements, demonstrated in the public arena of equal opportunity.

As I grew up, I believed that my father's formula for success would pay off. Like many other Americans of Asian descent, I did pretty well in school and went on to an Ivy League university. It was only when I arrived at Dartmouth College in the fall of 1985 that I realized that equal opportunity was not necessarily what my father had thought it was. During the next four years my perceptions of equality and fairness were strongly challenged. I had come to a place where professors, radical students, and professional charlatans turned reality on its head, where the *lingua franca* contained words like: white male patriarchy, ethnocentricity, Eurocentrism, diversity, heterosexism, pluralism, ethnoviolence, community, phallocracy, oppressive structures, and reeducation.

The last word, reeducation, is quite descriptive of Dartmouth College's attempted relationship with its incoming freshman. For although I considered myself only partially educated when I arrived at Dartmouth, it seemed that I was already in need of reeducation because I didn't quite know the rules of the game. Although I was a woman, I didn't perceive the widespread sexism that campus feminists and female professors assured me was all around. Although I was a member of a minority group, I didn't particularly feel any solidarity with the various ethnic groups claiming special victim status and demanding special programs and perks for themselves. And most telling of all, I was actually surprised to find that whereas I had always taken race and ethnic status for granted before, at Dartmouth everyone from the students to the faculty to the administrators to the village bums -- they all seemed intimately preoccupied with race and affirmative action. Everyone, that is, but the incoming freshmen, and they quickly learned to categorize themselves according to whether they were oppressors or oppressed, privileged or deprived, socially conscious or, like myself, in need of sensitivity training.

But I had come to Dartmouth for an education, not a sociopolitical reeducation. The fact that Dartmouth's radical *Weltanshauung*, its challenged and patronizing assumptions about minority handicaps and entitlements, and its overt attempts at didactic mind control went unquestioned by any campus leaders, the daily student paper, or any vocal source outside the university, eventually led me to join the staff of *The Dartmouth Review*, then the only voice at Dartmouth attempting to reverse the hidebound orthodoxy of the college.

Founded in 1980 as a much-needed antidote to the College's house organs of news information, *The Dartmouth Review* sought to fight the party line with a weekly combination of hard reporting, sharp editorials, and provocative humor in the form of satire. A radical activist in the '60s might have called what the *Review* tries to do "maximizing the contradictions." Many of the *Review*'s journalistic forays have embroiled it in heated controversy, and the paper's editors have often been the targets of attempts by school administrators to expel or suspend them for articles they have written.

As a contributor to *The Dartmouth Review*, I learned some hard facts about the intellectual monopoly on the topic of race. It seems that whenever a conservative tries to broach the topic of race, be it in relation to quotas, affirmative action, apartheid, or any of a host of social issues, he or she is immediately confronted with the reality that most liberals, and especially the doctrinaire type now found only on American campuses, find the topic of race to be their exclusive domain. Indeed, the arguments used or even the race of the individual doing the questioning makes no difference. One classmate of mine on the *Review* staff, who happened to have committed the double sin of being conservative and black, was burned in effigy outside the headquarters of the divestment movement during our freshman year. Other minority staffers have received death threats, sometimes in the presence of professors who are complicit in their silence. And these things should come as no surprise, really, because the hero of Dartmouth's minorities today is not Martin Luther King, or even Mahatma K. Gandhi. The hero is Malcolm X, evidenced by the fact that a huge mural depicting him dominates the entrance to Cutter Hall, headquarters of the Afro-American society. And the International Students organization, which can always be counted on to confuse its Third World grievances with the incessant demands of other victim pressure groups, recently changed the name of its headquarters, once named after an early president of Dartmouth, to the Fidel Castro House. So violence, heavyhanded intimidation, and leftism tend to go hand in hand at my alma mater.

The *cri de coeur* of Dartmouth's orthodoxy is "diversity," a word that immediately signals to the listener that someone is about to begin preaching to the choir. Dartmouth's President James Freedman likes to refer to his dream of Dartmouth as a pluralism of otherness. (He's a Harvard man, so his circumloquacity and pomposity are perhaps understandable.) Questioning the amorphous and criminally overused symbolism of diversity or raising impolite questions about the intellectual integrity of minority quotas, the "paint-by-numbers" approach to achieving "diversity," is tantamount to committing blasphemy against the state religion. To point out the self-segregation in dormitories, fraternities, and sororities, to notice the separate black and white tables in the dining halls, to observe the spiraling tensions created by escalating demands from pressure groups -- to make note of these facts is to invite villification, is to beg to be labeled with the McCarthyist labels of "racist" and "fascist." Speaking out on the topic of race guarantees that no black friend of yours who wants to be accepted by the black establishment on the campus will be able to resist the pressure from his black peers to sever your friendship.

A fine example of how racial hysteria can obfuscate and hijack completely non-racial issues is the so-called "Cole" incident. Professor William Cole, a jazz musician, taught a course at Dartmouth officially entitled "Music in the Oral Tradition", better known as the most blatant "gut" in the entire curriculum. In 1984 the newspaper did its first expose of Cole, observing that his lectures consisted mainly of soliloquies about urban reality, Cole's difficult-to-describe personal philosophy about life, white conspiracies to "get" blacks, and frequent diatribes against "honkies," many of whom were taking the class. The *Review* revealed that Cole devoted little attention to music and required little from his students other than their acquiescence in his lax teaching style, rarely assigning reading or graded writing exercises. No one has ever disputed the accuracy of the article, but faculty members immediately accused the *Review* of racism for critically examining the class because, of course, Cole happens to be black. Although Cole's race was neither an issue in the article nor a factor in the decision to expose his class, liberals immediately joined Cole in postulating a causal link between his race and the article.

The evening the issue containing the article was distributed, Cole went to the dorm room of Laura Ingraham, the editor of the newspaper, banged on the door for 20 minutes, and screamed unprintable obscenities about her in the hallway. Ingraham was not home but her roommate, terrified at the frenzied behavior of the professor, called the campus police and reported the incident. Despite these unprofessional outbursts, Cole was not punished by the college; in fact, his actions were defended as justified by the dean of the faculty. He accused the newspaper of libel and sued it for two million dollars, although his suit was later thrown out of court for lack of evidence.

The newspaper's second, more spectacular run-in with the professor came in February of 1988. One snowy afternoon two freshmen trudged into the Main Street offices of the newspaper and asked to talk to the editor, who at that time was junior Christopher Baldwin. One of the students told Baldwin that he wanted the newspaper to investigate Professor Cole's teaching style and class content, not knowing of the paper's attempt to do the same thing four years earlier. The student had been ordered by Cole not to come to class wearing his Indian t-shirt, a free welcome gift given to all freshmen by the newspaper in an attempt to keep the school's traditional but now banned symbol alive. Baldwin had coincidentally just been asked by another freshman to investigate the similarly content-free introductory English class being taught by a white professor, and decided to do a double investigation.

The articles on the English professor and Cole were prominently featured together in an issue of the newspaper, and the article about Cole contained a transcript of one of his classes given to the newspaper by a student, a transcript so devastatingly revealing in itself that the newspaper hardly needed any additional comment to prove the point that the college was taking students for a ride by giving them credit for the course. Because of Cole's earlier lawsuit against the newspaper, the *Review*'s lawyers advised Baldwin that the two professors should be invited to respond, unedited, to the charges made about their classroom performances. The English professor's supervisor replied to the paper, promising that changes would be made in the content and requirements of the course.

When Cole, on the other hand, failed to respond several days after the first article appeared, Baldwin, two other staffers and a photographer went to the room where he holds class and waited outside until the class was over; their purpose was to deliver to him a written invitation to respond. When they went in to deliver the invitation, however, they got a lot more than what they had bargained for. Cole immediately erupted into a string of obscenities and began poking his fingers at Baldwin's eyes. The *Review* photographer naturally began taking photos of this, and the tape recorder was running to record it as well. Cole then lunged at the photographer and ripped off the flash attachment of his camera, hurling it to the floor and destroying it. The tape indicates that the students throughout addressed Cole as "sir," while he unleashed at them a nonstop stream of obscenities. When the professor noticed the tape recorder he asked the students to leave, which they promptly did. The next issue of the *Review* contained three photographs of the incident and a complete transcript of the three minute encounter. The very same day, campus police delivered notices to the students that they were to stand trial for invasion of privacy, disorderly conduct, and harrassment.

In fact, the editors met Cole in a public auditorium, after his class was dismissed, and took the tools of the trade with them to clearly indicate their journalistic purpose. In fact, the Review writers behaved no differently in pursuit of their story than Mike Wallace might behave if investigating a hostile subject for a *60 Minutes* segment.

But Mike Wallace happens to be protected by the Bill of Rights, whereas college counsel Sean Gorman has often noted, with some satisfaction, that Dartmouth, as a private institution, can easily pretend that the Bill of Rights simply doesn't exist. Soon after the students were charged, Dartmouth president James Freedman, responding to a mob camped outside administration headquarters, summarily pronounced the *Review* four guilty even before their trial, denouncing their behavior as "meanspirited, cruel and ugly," and incidentally proclaiming Cole to be an invaluable asset to the international jazz community. At a hearing chaired by the Dean of the College, the four staffers (who were denied counsel and the right to cross-examine witnesses, among other things) were found guilty of the three charges against them and, in addition, were convicted of a new charge, "vexatious oral exchange," which sounds like some kind of morals charge, but is actually a bureaucratic neologism meaning that the students had argued with Cole. Editor Baldwin and the paper's senior editor were suspended for a year and a half, the photographer for three terms, and the other staff given a year's probation. And what of Cole? Although many of his colleagues privately acknowledged that he was an embarassment to the College, publicly the lionization of him reached ridiculous heights, and any faculty who questioned whether the professor might not also be at fault were themselves labeled racists. Professor of English Jeffrey Hart, who is also a senior editor at *National Review* and the lone outspoken conservative on the Dartmouth faculty, was condemned at a faculty meeting for his previous support of the student newspaper.

Ironically, in attempting to shut down the newspaper by attacking its leadership, Dartmouth's liberal establishment drew upon itself scorn from liberals and conservatives around the nation. Joining several Congressmen, Senators, and cabinet officials in condemning the college's administration were the American Civil Liberties Union and such leading lights of the free speech lobby as Alan Dershowitz and Nat Hentoff. Even *The Washington Post* published an editorial critical of the college's abrogation of free speech and freedom of the press. The *Review* filed a lawsuit against Dartmouth immediately following the incident, and a New Hampshire state judge ordered Dartmouth to reverse the suspensions because the "trial" had been fundamentally unfair, and the charges against the students unproven. The issue of damages to be paid to them by the College is still pending. And this, I might add, is only one of many such incidents between the *Review* and the College's self-proclaimed arbiters of acceptable thought. Other lawsuits continued to wind their ways through the courts.

The Dartmouth Review is lucky. Financially and legally independent of the College, the beneficiary of loyal alumni and conservative supporters around the country, it could hire top-rank New York attorneys and publicists. But most other campus papers or independent students with iconoclastic views on affirmative action and victim studies departments are not usually in such an advantageous position. The threat of university action scares most students away from speaking their minds. Papers like *The Vassar Spectator*, which similarly tried to expose hypocrisy and anti-Semitism on the part of a black student activist, quickly find their budgets withdrawn, their offices closed, and their school records permanently blemished.

And these threats are not isolated or rare. In the past 18 months regulations barring free speech, or ad hoc attempts to suppress student newspapers, have appeared at Stanford, Emory, Brown, Arizona State, Berkeley, the University of North Carolina at Chapel Hill, UCLA, The State University at Northridge, and several others -- the list grows longer every day.

And who, after all, are the real victims of the liberal stranglehold on the issue of race? White students may suffer, but talented ones will usually find a good school to accept them, although it may not be the school of their first choice. Asian students may find it harder to get into the top schools, since they must unfairly compete against other Asians for their seats -- but they, too, will generally excel wherever they are accepted and overcome the restrictions placed on them by affirmative action. I think that the real victims of affirmative action are the minority students the quota system was set up to help.

The ones who are very intelligent, and who would have been admitted without affirmative action, suffer the same taint of doubt about their right to be there as the students who are marginally qualified, and benefitted from relaxed standards. Although their achievements brought them to a top school, their color keeps them from being accepted for what they are, and if they are accepted, and welcomed into the mainstream of campus life, they can be assured of taunts from other minority students -- they will be called "oreos" -- black on the outside, white on the inside -- or "incogs" short for incog-negro. Too often, as a result of this peer pressure that makes them question whether they have betrayed their people, they become the most articulate defenders of affirmative action, issuing the most passionate denials against the fact that affirmative action constitutes double standards. They perpetuate the hoax, paradoxically further degrading the legitimacy of their minority peers in the eyes of the mainstream.

And then there are the students who are admitted by virtue of relaxed standards. I do not exaggerate when I say that many minority students struggle through their first year or two at Dartmouth simply playing catch-up, sitting through remedial or slower track English and mathematics courses, while other students clear their distributive requirements out of the way and move on to more advanced study. When it comes time to pick a major or concentration, many minority students, ill-prepared for a major in physics or classical studies, opt for the easy way out, concentrations in the victim genres of Afro-American, Women's, and Native American Studies, disciplines distinguished mainly for their lack of discipline, their vague imputations of aggrievement, their all-consuming crusades to rewrite history. Suffice it to say that 10 or 15 years from now, these students may consider their choices of study ill-considered. And Dartmouth has really done them no favor by taking them in unprepared and pushing them out again, four years later, arguably no less behind the curve than they were before.

The other sad legacy of the divisive politics of race is the creation of racism, or at least indelible feelings of bitterness and resentment, where no such sentiments previously existed. An example comes to mind: after the Cole incident, a coalition of minority groups and leftist professors called a rally on the steps of the administration building, in order to bring pressure to bear on the President, who was being urged to condemn the four *Review* students. Our paper sent a reporter and a photographer to cover the event, but a freshman wanted to tag along as well, just to see what the protest would be like, and naively, to share his own views and feelings with some members of the crowd, hoping that he would learn something, and so would they. The student, whose family emigrated from Korea in the mid-'80s, tried to explain to one black activist toting a sign saying "Expel the Racists" why the accused criminals were not, in fact, racists, but were actually pretty decent human beings. The black radical, after stonily looking in the other direction, impatiently turned and angrily brushed the freshman aside, sneering, "What the hell do you know about racism? You just got off the banana boat, buddy,"

In the short term, will restrictions on the press and on free and open discussion of race-related issues on our nation's campuses protect the vulnerable feelings of minorities? Perhaps. But do they allow the university to fulfill its historical role as a temple of truth, as a refuge from the pedestrian pressures of party politics, as, above all, a place where the quest for knowledge is the supreme and defining value? We can each judge for ourselves whether feelings should triumph over hard facts, but there simply has to be a better way to offer the best opportunities to all Americans who want and deserve them. Perhaps one day we will all agree that openness, and a free exchange of thoughts and ideas ultimately leading to a better understanding of one other, is better than the silence and organized deceit that now passes for constructive dialogue on the issue of race.

10

The Saliency of Race

Glenn Loury

Let me begin by saying, at a conference entitled "Second Thoughts on Race" that I don't have any. I am a black man, and plan on staying that way. That is one part of my Sixties heritage that I do not intend to go back on. As an American, even if I wanted to escape the implications of race it would be impossible. We Americans, black and white, all have to confront the saliency, the power, the inescapability of race. There is a sense in which this is a fundamentally racialist, if not racist, society. After all, inter-marriage rates are not that high. Segregated residential communities are still widely observed. And, in our own lives, in the sphere of associations that define our personal identities, in our own social behavior, we make racial distinctions readily, daily, in terms of whom we befriend and whom we embrace. These personal decisions of association ought not to be the subject of legislation or, necessarily, of moral approbation, but they are nevertheless a reflection of the saliency of race in our social lives.

So we Americans are stuck with the race question. We're going to be confronting it for a long time. We are heirs of an ambiguous legacy -- the idea of free self government bequeathed us by the Founding Fathers, and now the envy and goal of all the world, but also the legacy of a slave society. In our midst, among us, before you, are the descendants of people who were property. This is a point that is much abused -- "four hundred years of slavery" is the typical formulation. It has become a touchstone of the complaint industry, of the "professional black," of the guilt mongerer. Nevertheless it is good to start with this historical fact. We do well to reflect upon it. We ought not try to get away from it. For this legacy of slavery, this incompleteness today of the process begun with the Emancipation, this continuing struggle to create a common civic life for all Americans -- it is this that brings us together here today. This legacy makes black Americans unique among minority claimants. This history of subjugation, violence, dehumanization, alienation, and the efforts to legitimize and rationalize it in a Christian Democracy -- this is where racism, or if you prefer racialism, as it relates to blacks, is born.

And so, we are all racialists now. Convened here as we are to have our "Second Thoughts" about race, we do well to remember that no one in America is truly "color-blind." The very fact that I stand here before you -- a black neoconservative -- being praised and honored for the courage to "do the right (wing) thing", even as I am branded a traitor by many blacks, reveals the inescapable power of race in our political lives today. And those of you who are former radicals, now engaged in rethinking old racial truths in light of the intervening failures and disappointments, would have it no other way. My breaking ranks confirms your "apostasy" as valid, and non-racist, because I am black. If by some magic I became white, my "brilliant, perceptive, courageous" insights would suddenly become pedestrian commonplace complaints, and would be of little political or personal comfort to you.

That being the case, it is incumbent upon me to remind you that, while we are having and must have some second and third thoughts about race, while we must think hard and be honest and truthful and try to analyze what has gone wrong and figure out where to go, let us not lose sight of the fact that there was and remains a reason for a thrust toward reform. There was and remains good ground for a movement whose goal is the attainment of racial justice. The issue then and now is not getting beyond racial justice. The issue is how do we deliver it. What do we do about it?

The so-called "underclass" is the racial problem of our time. It constitutes a fundamental moral challenge to us. It represents the major unfinished business of the struggle for racial justice. The fact that this problem is shamelessly exploited by opportunistic charlatans whose programs of reform relate little to the genuine malady and who in a self-promoting fashion and in ever-more aggressive ways offer non-solutions; the fact that demagogues use this problem as grist for their mills, that cowardly politicians point to it and then posture vis-a-vis it in order to garner for themselves some moral bona fides by virtue of having done the right thing with respect to it, when in fact they've done nothing at all; the fact that this is the case does not relieve us of the responsibility of being engaged with it.

We're not off the hook because *they* are crazy. Do you understand what I'm saying? We have to get beyond complaint and a litany of their wrongs. We have to find constructive and positive things to say and do about the problems of racial justice around us. For we are becoming two America's now. I know that you do not expect to hear this from me. You do not expect me to decry the terrible homelessness that exists. But it is, after all, pretty bad in some places. You don't expect to hear from me about how a black kid born in a certain social context has poorer chances of succeeding in life than a white kid born in another context. But in fact so many black kids' chances, actual life chances, are so miserable that fundamental questions of justice, racial justice, are raised.

The infant mortality rate is a problem. And let us by all means observe that the infant mortality rate is not due to racism. And yet after we have observed that, after we have observed that the crack epidemic and the violence which accompanies it is not due to racism of any remediable sort that the Civil Rights Act is going to get at; after we've done that, then I think we have to start talking about what we are going to do about the infant mortality problem. It is a complicated problem, and in a city like Washington, D.C., it is inescapably a racial problem as well. It is not simply a problem of spending money, but the issue of spending this or that many millions of dollars on infant mortality really ought not to delay us very long, if as people who seek justice we are appropriately motivated by our sense of outrage at the condition.

We ought to be able to keep two or three ideas in our heads at the same time. The demagogues on the left have it wrong. That's one idea. A large part of America is going to hell in a handbasket. That is another idea and there's absolutely no doubt about it. We sit here now just a couple of miles from it. Let's not lose sight of that. We have a moral responsibility to do something about it. Us, you and me, whatever our political persuasion. The issue is: how are we going to proceed? So while we are decrying how the Civil Rights movement has been captured by the crazies, let us not lose sight of that issue.

The problems of the inner-city poor are not our only racial problem, however. Race is salient on the campus as well. I was at Vassar College not long ago giving a talk. It was a standard sort of situation. I had been invited by the "conservative" students. They turned out not to be conservative at all. One of them had campaigned in high school for a Martin Luther King Day celebration, which helped her get admitted to Vassar. Another thought Fay Wattleton of Planned Parenthood was a great heroine. A third argued with me that the welfare state should be bigger than it is and so forth. What made them conservatives at Vassar was the fact that they were three who were prepared to speak out against the politically correct line, especially on racial issues.

I gave my talk to a segregated audience. Self-segregated. The white kids sat over here and the black kids sat over there. And, whenever I said we blacks must affirm universal ideals, we have to rely upon self-help, we have to stop whining and start building, cheers rang out from the mostly white, "conservative" part of the audience -- interrupted by applause -- while the blacks seethed, shifting uncomfortably in their seats. Waiting for their turn. Their turn, I'm sad to have to report, was during the Q and A. They let me have it; they did not even try to conceal their hostility. I had dared to use the first person plural to refer to the body of people who constitute the citizenry of the United States. We, our, us. "Don't you know that *we* weren't there at the Constitutional convention? We were three-fifths of a man."

Now that's not just the rant of some poorly educated kid. You can listen to Supreme Court justices agree. You can hear law professors reaffirm it. And then the chant "Yusef Hawkins" started ringing out -- almost literally a chant. "Yusef Hawkins." I had dared to say that you can do anything in America. I had asked people to try to place some kind of historical perspective on what exactly it meant to be an undergraduate at Vassar College in 1990. Anything is possible. We are the most privileged, empowered black people, people of African descent, anywhere on the globe, I had said. All things are possible. We must not take on this self-limiting mantle of "I'm just a black and I'm oppressed." I said this to the young people and they started chanting "Yusef Hawkins." Didn't I know that the fact that Yusef Hawkins had been shot down in Bensonhurst cancelled out everything? That that fact made it impossible for them to envision the reality of achieving?

This experience at Vassar included a white professor of Chinese studies coming up to me, earnestly shaking my hand, commending me for my "courage," and asking "Do you know Tom Sowell?" As I said, we are all racialists. Do you see my point? We don't get away from the race thing. Race is right there; it's the salient category. It's always just beneath the surface. This professor of Chinese studies wanted so desperately not to be condemned as a racist that he looked to me for deliverance. He sees personified before him courage and license. I'm going to make it O.K. Tom Sowell and I will come riding in, battle-scarred, to say that all is well, and to tell the runny-nosed black kids who have been tyrannizing these well-meaning white liberals to go to hell.

My visit also included learning about the experience of a youngster, a black at Vassar, who was driven off the campus by the administration, had financial aid cancelled at the last minute just before finals, and received a letter telling him that four thousand dollars was due in tuition that his folks couldn't pay, because he had dared to join the conservative club and start showing up with a suit and bow-tie. You know how we -- they -- dress. He dared to start showing up in his suit and bow-tie and some black came up to him at a function and took his arm and started rubbing his skin, saying "I'm sure that is going to rub off and we're going to find a white man underneath." When the student complained about it the retort from the administration in part was "You provoked this by being part of that club and wearing that suit." One complaint led to another and the next thing you know, so I'm told by the "conservative" students, this student was driven off campus.

I thought of all these things as I stood looking out at this segregated audience. Here is this one black kid telling me he's three-fifths of a person. Here are these "conservative" whites cheering every time I tell black people the things that they -- we -- really do need to hear. And I start thinking this race thing is deep. This is now beyond good advice. And I started asking myself -- well, I'm trained as an economic theorist, what the hell am I doing here? How did I get to this point of brokerage, to this juncture of conflict?

I realized that the saliency and the power and the depth of race was such in our society that it had compelled me there, that to a certain extent I was -- I am -- trapped. *We* are trapped, and there is not any easy way out of it. There is not any talking my way out of it. There is not any "ideologizing" my way out of it. This is the great temptation that we Americans must all resist: that we can escape the dilemmas and discomforts of race by embracing some great transcendent truth; some fundamental principle. We can become advocates of a "color-blind society." We can urge that the black poor must take "personal responsibility." We can discover that all our efforts to help simply made things worse. Or, we can find in "white racism" the cause of all our troubles.

But we are not going to get free of this "race thing" by finding an idea, whatever it may be -- a libertarian or an ultramarxist lens -- through which the world suddenly looks simple. No system will adequately explain this. No incantation of a slogan is going to free us of it. We are in this thing together, caught up in a historical dynamic that goes back centuries. And we are going to have to work our way out of it. And in order to work our way out of it we're going to have to talk candidly with each other about it. We're going to have to create the space, without having to pay obeisance to the politically-correct line every time we open our mouths, without having to look over our shoulders, running scared at the prospect that we might be called racists.

Yes, that requires courage from people like us. But it also requires some courage and change by the major institutions in this society, including the presidency, which notwithstanding the fact that it is in the hands of Republicans often runs when the chance for real national leadership on these issues presents itself. And it will require courage from the press. I was dismayed to pick up the *New York Times* after the City Councilman in Milwaukee called for urban guerilla warfare, and to read their editorial. I was astounded; I could not believe it. That editorial said, in effect, that we should understand the conditions in Milwaukee's black ghetto that provoked such a statement. Those conditions are very bad. I have already said that we must address those conditions. But the fact of the matter is that if an elected public official calls for urban guerilla warfare, he deserves to be condemned.

When the *Times* takes the easy way out, saying in effect, "Oh well, we must not offend sensibilities," in the face of a clear affront to common values worthy of defense, it either exhibits a lack of respect for the importance of those values, or it shows its racism by virtue of considering the councilman insufficiently worthy of their attention and concern to be confronted with their genuine judgments regarding his behavior. As a member of Harvard University's faculty, I know something about this. I know how people posture; how they see inside of what's going on. And yet they sit quietly and wait for me (a man of courage) to do their work. Well, I'm tired of doing y'alls work.

Part III

Standards and Double Standards

Shelby Steele

Abigail Thernstrom

Henry Mark Holzer

11

The Recoloring of Campus Life

Shelby Steele

In the past few years, we have witnessed what the National Institute Against Prejudice and Violence calls a "proliferation" of racial incidents on college campuses around the country. Incidents of on-campus "intergroup conflict" have occurred at more than 160 colleges in the last three years, according to the Institute. The nature of these incidents has ranged from open racial violence -- most notoriously, the October 1986 beating of a black student at the University of Massachusetts at Amherst after an argument about the World Series turned into a racial bashing, with a crowd of up to 3,000 whites chasing 20 blacks -- to the harassment of minority students, to acts of racial or ethnic insensitivity, with by far the greatest number falling in the last two categories. At Dartmouth College, three editors of the *Dartmouth Review*, the off-campus right-wing student weekly, were suspended last winter for harassing a black professor in his lecture hall. At Yale University last year a swastika and the words "white power" were painted on the school's Afro-American cultural center. Racist jokes were aired not long ago on a campus radio station at the University of Michigan. And at the University of Wisconsin at Madison, members of the Zeta Beta Tau fraternity held a mock slave auction in which pledges painted their faces black and wore Afro wigs. Two weeks after the President of Stanford University informed the incoming freshmen class last fall that "bigotry is out, and I mean it," two freshmen defaced a poster of Beethoven -- gave the image thick lips -- and hung it on a black student's door.

The Recoloring of Campus Life orignally appeared in **Harper's Magazine**, February 1989.

In response, black students around the country have rediscovered the militant protest strategies of the '60s. At the University of Massachusetts at Amherst, Williams College, Penn State University, UC Berkeley, UCLA, Stanford, and countless other campuses, black students have sat in, marched, and rallied. But much of what they were marching and rallying about seemed less a response to specific racial incidents than a call for broader action on the part of the colleges and universities they were attending. Black students have demanded everything from more black faculty members and new courses on racism to the addition of "ethnic" foods in the cafeteria. There is the sense in these demands that racism runs deep.

Of course, universities are not where racial problems tend to arise. When I went to college in the mid-'60s, colleges were oases of calm and understanding in a racially tense society; campus life -- with its traditions of tolerance and fairness, its very distance from the "real" world -- imposed a degree of broad-mindedness on even the most provincial students. If I met whites who were not anxious to be friends with blacks, most were at least vaguely friendly to the cause of our freedom. In any case, there was no guerilla activity against our presence, no "mine field of racism" (as one black student at Berkeley recently put it) to negotiate. I wouldn't say that the phrase "campus racism" is a contradiction in terms, but until recently it certainly seemed an incongruence.

But a greater incongruence is the generational timing of this new problem on the campuses. Today's undergraduates were born after the passage of the 1964 Civil Rights Act. They grew up in an age when racial equality was for the first time enforceable by law. This too was a time when blacks suddenly appeared on television, as mayors of big cities, as icons of popular culture, as teachers, and in some cases even as neighbors. Today's black and white college students, veterans of *Sesame Street* and often of integrated grammar and high schools, have had more opportunities to know each other -- whites and blacks -- than any previous generation in American history. Not enough opportunities, perhaps, but enough to make the notion of racial tension on campus something of a mystery, at least to me.

To try to unravel this mystery I left my own campus, where there have been few signs of racial tension, and talked with black and white students at California schools where racial incidents had occurred: Stanford, UCLA, Berkeley. I spoke with black and white students -- and not with Asians and Hispanics -- because, as always, blacks and whites represent the deepest lines of division, and because I hesitate to wander onto the complex territory of other minority groups. A phrase by William H. Gass -- "the hidden internality of things" -- describes with maybe a little too much grandeur what I hoped to find. But it is what I wanted to find, for this is the kind of problem that makes a black person nervous, which is not to say that it doesn't unnerve whites as well. Once every six months or so someone yells "nigger" at me from a passing car. I don't like to think that these solo artists might soon make up a chorus or, worse, that this chorus might one day soon sing to me from the paths of my own campus.

I have long believed that trouble between races is seldom what it appears to be. It was not hard to see after my first talks with students that racial tension on campus is a problem that misrepresents itself. It has the same look, the archetypical pattern, of America's timeless racial conflict -- white racism and black protest. And I think part of our concern over it comes from the fact that it has the feel of a relapse, illness gone and come again. But if we are seeing the same symptoms, I don't believe we are dealing with the same illness. For one thing, I think racial tension on campus is the result more of racial equality than inequality.

How to live with racial difference has been America's profound social problem. For the first 100 years or so following emancipation it was controlled by a legally sanctioned inequality that acted as a buffer between the races. No longer is this the case. On campuses today, as throughout society, blacks enjoy equality under the law -- a profound social advancement. No student may be kept out of a class or a dormitory or an extracurricular activity because of his or her race. But there is a paradox here: On a campus where members of all races are gathered, mixed together in the classroom as well as socially, differences are more exposed than ever. And this is where the trouble starts. For members of each race -- young adults coming into their own, often away from home for the first time -- bring to this site of freedom, exploration, and now, today, equality, very deep fears and anxieties, inchoate feelings of racial shame, anger, and guilt. These feelings could lie dormant in the home, in familiar neighborhoods, in simpler days of childhood. But the college campus, with its structures of interaction and adult-level competition -- the big exam, the dorm, the "mixer" -- is another matter. I think campus racism is born of the rub between racial difference and a setting, the campus itself, devoted to interaction and equality. On our campuses, such concentrated micro-societies, all that remains unresolved between blacks and whites, all the old wounds and shames that have never been addressed, present themselves for attention -- and present our youth with pressures they cannot always handle.

I have mentioned one paradox: racial fears and anxieties among blacks and whites bubbling up in an era of racial equality under the law, in settings that are among the freest and fairest in society. And there is another, related paradox, stemming from the notion of -- and practice of -- affirmative action. Under the provisions of the Equal Employment Opportunity Act of 1972, all state governments and institutions (including universities) were forced to initiate plans to increase the proportion of minority and women employees -- in the case of universities, of students too. Affirmative action plans that establish racial quotas were ruled unconstitutional more than ten years ago in *University of California v. Bakke*. But quotas are only the most controversial aspect of affirmative action; the principle of affirmative action is reflected in various university programs aimed at redressing and overcoming past patterns of discrimination. Of course, to be conscious of patterns of discrimination -- the fact, say, that public schools in the black inner cities are more crowded and employ fewer top-notch teachers than white suburban public schools, and that this is a factor in student performance -- is only reasonable. However, in doing this we also call attention quite obviously to difference: in the case of blacks and whites, racial difference. What has emerged on campus in recent years -- as a result of progress -- is a *politics of difference*, a troubling, volatile politics in which each group justifies itself, its sense of worth and its pursuit of power, through difference alone.

In this context, racial, ethnic, and gender differences become forms of sovereignty, campuses become balkanized, and each group fights with whatever means are available. No doubt there are many factors that have contributed to the rise of racial tension on campus: What has been the role of fraternities, which have returned to campus with their inclusions and exclusions? What role has the heightened notion of college as some first step to personal, financial success played in increasing competition, and thus tension? Mostly what I sense, though, is that in interactive settings, while fighting the fights of "difference," old ghosts are stirred, and haunt again. Black and white Americans simply have the power to make each other feel shame and guilt. In the "real" world, we may be able to deny these feelings, keep them at bay. But these feelings are likely to surface on college campuses, where young people are groping for identity and power, and where difference is made to matter so greatly. In a way, racial tension on campus in the '80s might have been inevitable.

I would like, first, to discuss black students, their anxieties and vulnerabilities. The accusation that black Americans have always lived with is that they are inferior -- inferior simply because they are black. And this accusation has been too uniform, too ingrained in cultural imagery, too enforced by law, custom, and every form of power not to have left a mark. Black inferiority was a precept accepted by the founders of this nation; it was a principle of social organization that relegated blacks to the sidelines of American life. So when today's young black students find themselves on white campuses, surrounded by those who historically have claimed superiority, they are also surrounded by the myth of their inferiority.

Of course it is true that many young people come to college with some anxiety about not being good enough. But only blacks come wearing a color that is still, in the minds of some, a sign of inferiority. Poles, Jews, Hispanics, and other groups also endure degrading stereotypes. But two things make the myth of black inferiority a far heavier burden: the broadness of its scope and its incarnation in color. There are not only more stereotypes of blacks than of other groups, but these stereotypes are also more dehumanizing, more focused on the most despised of human traits - stupidity, laziness, sexual immorality, dirtiness, and so on. In America's racial and ethnic hierarchy, blacks have clearly been relegated to the lowest level -- have been burdened with an ambiguous, animalistic humanity. Moreover, this is made unavoidable for blacks by the sheer visibility of black skin, a skin that evokes the myth of inferiority on sight. And today this myth is sadly reinforced for many black students by affirmative action programs, under which blacks may often enter college with lower test scores and high-school grade point averages than whites. "They see me as an affirmative action case," one black student told me at UCLA.

So when a black student enters college, the myth of inferiority compounds the normal anxiousness over whether he or she will be good enough. This anxiety is not only personal but also racial. The families of these students will have pounded into them the fact that blacks are not inferior. And probably more than anything, it is this pounding that finally leaves a mark. If I am not inferior, why the need to say so?

This myth of inferiority constitutes a very sharp and ongoing anxiety for young blacks, the nature of which is very precise: It is the terror that somehow, through one's actions or by virtue of some "proof" (a poor grade, a flubbed response in class), one's fear of inferiority -- inculcated in ways large and small by society -- will be confirmed as real. On a university campus, where intelligence itself is the ultimate measure, this anxiety is bound to be triggered.

A black student I met at UCLA was disturbed a little when I asked him if he ever felt vulnerable -- anxious about "black inferiority" -- as a black student. But after a long pause, he finally said, "I think I do". The example he gave was of a large lecture class he'd taken with more than 300 students. Fifty or so black students sat in the back of the lecture hall and "acted out every stereotype in the book". They were loud, ate food, came in late - and generally got lower grades than the whites in the class. "I knew I would be seen like them, and I didn't like it. I never sat by them". Seen like what? I asked, though we both knew the answer. "As lazy, ignorant, and stupid," he said sadly.

Had the group at the back been white fraternity brothers, they would not have been seen as dumb *whites*, of course. And a frat brother who worried about his grades would not worry that he would be seen "like them". The terror in this situation for the student I spoke with was that his own deeply buried anxiety would be given credence, that the myth would be verified, and that he would feel shame and humiliation not because of who he was but simply because he was black. In this lecture hall his race, quite apart from his performance, might subject him to four unendurable feelings -- diminishment, accountability to the preconceptions of whites, a powerlessness to change those preconceptions, and, finally, shame. These are the feelings that make up his racial anxiety, and that of all blacks on any campus. On a white campus a black is never far from these feelings, and even his unconscious knowledge that he is subject to them can undermine his self-esteem. There are blacks on every campus who are not up to doing good college-level work. Certain black students may not be happy or motivated or in the appropriate field of study - *just like whites.* (Let us not forget that many white students get poor grades, fail, drop out.) Moreover, many more blacks than whites are not quite prepared for college, may have to catch up, owing to factors beyond their control: poor previous schooling, for example. But the white who has to catch up will not be anxious that his being behind is a matter of his whiteness, of his being *racially* inferior. The black student may well have such a fear.

This, I believe, is one reason why black colleges in America turn out 34 percent of all black college graduates, though they enroll only 17 percent of black college students. Without whites around on campus the myth of inferiority is in abeyance and, along with it, a great reservoir of culturally imposed self-doubt. On black campuses feelings of inferiority are personal; on campuses with a white majority, a black's problems have a way of becoming a "black" problem.

But this feeling of vulnerability a black may feel in itself is not as serious a problem as what he or she does with it. To admit that one is made anxious in integrated situations about the myth of racial inferiority is difficult for young blacks. It seems like admitting that one *is* racially inferior. And so, most often, the student will deny harboring those feelings. This is where some of the pangs of racial tension begin, because denial always involves distortion.

In order to deny a problem we must tell ourselves that the problem is something different than what it really is. A black student at Berkeley told me that he felt defensive every time he walked into a class and saw mostly white faces. When I asked why, he said, "Because I know they're all racists. They think blacks are stupid." Of course it may be true that some whites feel this way, but the singular focus on white racism allows this student to obscure his own underlying racial anxiety. He can now say that his problem -- facing a class full of white faces, *fearing* that they think he is dumb -- is entirely the result of certifiable white racism and has nothing to do with his own anxieties, or even that this particular academic subject may not be his best. Now all the terror of his anxiety, its powerful energy, is devoted to simply *seeing* racism. Whatever evidence of racism he finds -- and looking this hard, he will no doubt find some -- can be brought in to buttress his distorted view of the problem, while his actual deep-seated anxiety goes unseen.

Denial, and the distortion that results, places the problem *outside* the self and in the world. It is not that I have any inferiority anxiety because of my race; it is that I am going to school with people who don't like blacks. This is the shift in thinking that allows black students to reenact the protest pattern of the '60s. Denied racial anxiety-distortion-reenactment is the process by which feelings of inferiority are transformed into an exaggerated white menace -- which is then protested against with the techniques of the past. Under the sway of this process, black students believe that history is repeating itself, that it's just like the '60s, or '50s. In fact, it is the not yet healed wounds from the past, rather than the inequality that created the wounds, that is the real problem.

This process generates an unconscious need to exaggerate the level of racism on campus -- to make it a matter of the system, not just a handful of students. Racism is the avenue away from the true inner anxiety. How many students demonstrating for a black "theme house" -- demonstrating in the style of the Sixties, when the battle was to win for blacks a place on campus -- might be better off spending their time reading and studying? Black students have the highest dropout rate and lowest grade point average of any group in American universities. This need not be so. And it is not the result of not having black theme houses.

It was my very good fortune to go to college in 1964, when the question of black "inferiority" was openly talked about among blacks. The summer before I left for college I heard Martin Luther King Jr. speak in Chicago, and he laid it on the line for black students everywhere. "When you are behind in a footrace, the only way to get ahead is to run faster than the man in front of you. So when your white roommate says he's tired and goes to sleep, you stay up and burn the midnight oil." His statement that we were "behind in a footrace" acknowledged that because of history, of few opportunities, of racism, we were, in a sense, "inferior". But this had to do with what had been done to our parents and their parents, not with inherent inferiority. And because it was acknowledged, it was presented to us as a challenge rather than a mark of shame.

Of the 18 black students (in a student body of 1,000) who were on campus in my freshman year, all graduated, though a number of us were not from the middle class. At the university where I currently teach, the drop-out rate for black students is 72 percent, despite the presence of several academic-support programs; a counseling center with black counselors; an Afro-American studies department; black faculty, administrators, and staff; a general education curriculum that emphasizes "cultural pluralism;" an Educational Opportunities Program; a mentor program; a black faculty and staff association; and an administration and faculty that often announce the need to do more for black students.

It may be unfair to compare my generation with the current one. Parents do this compulsively and to little end but self-congratulation. But I don't congratulate my generation. I think we were advantaged. We came along at a time when racial integration was held in high esteem. And integration was a very challenging social concept for both blacks and whites. We were remaking ourselves -- that's what one did at college -- and making history. We had something to prove. This was a profound advantage; it gave us clarity and a challenge. Achievement in the American mainstream was the goal of integration, and the best thing about this challenge was its secondary message -- that we *could* achieve.

There is much irony in the fact that black power would come along in the late '60s and change all of this. Black power was a movement of uplift and pride, and yet it also delivered the weight of pride -- a weight that would burden black students from then on. Black power "nationalized" the black identity, made blackness itself an object of celebration and allegiance. But if it transformed a mark of shame into a mark of pride, it also, in the name of pride, required the denial of racial anxiety. Without a frank account of one's anxieties, there is no clear direction, no concrete challenge. Black students today do not get as clear a message from their racial identity as my generation got. They are not filled with the same urgency to prove themselves, because black pride has said, "You're already proven, already equal, as good as anybody."

The "black identity" shaped by black power most powerfully contributes to racial tensions on campuses by basing entitlement more on race than on constitutional rights and standards of merit. With integration, black entitlement was derived from constitutional rights and standards of merit. With integration, black entitlement was derived from constitutional principles of fairness. Black power changed this by skewing the formula from rights of color -- if you were black, you were entitled. Thus, the United Coalition Against Racism (UCAR) at the University of Michigan could "demand" two years ago that all black professors be given immediate tenure, that there be special pay incentives for black professors, and that money be provided for an all-black student union. In this formula, black becomes the very color of entitlement, an extra right in itself, and a very dangerous grandiosity is promoted in which blackness amounts to specialness.

Race is, by any standard, an unprincipled source of power. And on campuses the use of racial power by one group makes racial or ethnic or gender *difference* a currency of power for all groups. When I make my difference into power, other groups must seize upon their difference to contain my power and maintain their position relative to me. Very quickly a kind of politics of difference emerges in which racial, ethnic, and gender groups are forced to assert their entitlement and vie for power based on the single quality that makes them different from one another.

On many campuses today academic departments and programs are established on the basis of difference -- black studies, women's studies, Asian studies, and so on -- despite the fact that there is nothing in these "difference" departments that cannot be studied within traditional academic disciplines. If their rationale truly is past exclusion from the mainstream curriculum, shouldn't the goal now be complete inclusion rather than separateness? I think this logic is overlooked because these groups are too interested in the power their difference can bring, and they insist on separate departments and programs as a tribute to that power.

This politics of difference makes everyone on campus a member of a minority group. It also makes racial tensions inevitable. To highlight one's difference as a source of advantage is also, indirectly, to inspire the enemies of that difference. When blackness (and femaleness) becomes a power, then white maleness is also sanctioned as power. A white male student at Stanford told me, "One of my friends said the other day that we should get together and start up a white student union and come up with a list of demands."

It is certainly true that white maleness has long been an unfair source of power. But the sin of white male power is precisely its use of race and gender as a source of entitlement. When minorities and women use their race, ethnicity, and gender in the same way, they not only commit the same sin but also, indirectly, sanction the very form of power that oppressed them in the first place. The politics of difference is based on a tit-for-tat sort of logic in which every victory only calls one's enemies to arms.

This elevation of difference undermines the communal impulse by making each group foreign and inaccessible to others. When difference is celebrated rather than remarked, people must think in terms of difference, they must find meaning in difference, and this meaning comes from an endless process of contrasting one's group with other groups. Blacks use whites to define themselves as different, women use men, Hispanics use whites and blacks, and on it goes. And in the process each group mythologizes and mystifies its difference, puts it beyond the full comprehension of outsiders. Difference becomes an inaccessible preciousness toward which outsiders are expected to be simply and uncomprehendingly reverential. But beware: In this world, even the insulated world of the college campus, preciousness is a balloon asking for a needle. At Smith College, graffiti appears: "Niggers, Spics, and Chinks quit complaining or get out."

Most of the white students I talked with spoke as if from under a faint cloud of accusation. There was always a ring of defensiveness in their complaints about blacks. A white student I spoke with at UCLA told me: "Most white students on this campus think the black student leadership here is made up of oversensitive crybabies who spend all their time looking for things to kick up a ruckus about." A white student at Stanford said: "Blacks do nothing but complain and ask for sympathy when everyone really knows they don't do well because they don't try. If they worked harder, they could do as well as everyone else."

That these students felt accused was most obvious in their compulsion to assure me that they were not racist. Oblique versions of some-of-my-best-friends-are stories came ritualistically before or after critiques of black students. Some said flatly, "I am not a racist, but..." Of course, we all deny being racists, but we only do this compulsively, I think, when we are working against an accusation of bias. I think it was the color of my skin, itself, that accused them.

This was the meta-message that surrounded these conversations like an aura, and in it, I believe, is the core of white American racial anxiety. My skin not only accused them, it judged them. And this judgment was a sad gift of history that brought them to account whether they deserved such an accounting or not. It said that wherever and whenever blacks were concerned, they had reason to feel guilt. And whether it was earned or unearned, I think it was guilt that set off the compulsion in these students to disclaim. I believe it is true that in America black people make white people feel guilty.

Guilt is the essence of white anxiety, just as inferiority is the essence of black anxiety. And the terror that it carries for whites is the terror of discovering that one has reason to feel guilt where blacks are concerned -- not so much because of what blacks might think but because of what guilt can say about oneself. If the darkest fear of blacks is inferiority, the darkest fear of whites is that their better lot in life is at least partially the result of their capacity for evil -- their capacity to dehumanize an entire people for their own benefit, and then to be indifferent to the devastation their dehumanization has wrought on successive generations of their victims. This is the terror that whites are vulnerable to regarding blacks. And the mere fact of being white is sufficient to feel it, since even whites with hearts clean of racism benefit from being white -- benefit at the expense of blacks. This is a conditional guilt having nothing to do with individual intentions or actions. And it makes for a very powerful anxiety because it threatens whites with a view of themselves as inhuman, just as inferiority threatens blacks with a similar view of themselves. At the dark core of both anxieties is a suspicion of incomplete humanity.

So the white students I met were not just meeting me; they were also meeting the possibility of their own inhumanity. And this, I think, is what explains how some young white college students in the late '80s can so frankly take part in racially insensitive and outright racist acts. They were expected to be cleaner of racism than any previous generation - they were born into the Great Society. But this expectation overlooks the fact that, for them, color is still an accusation and judgment. In black faces there is a discomforting reflection of white collective shame. Blacks remind them that their racial innocence is questionable, that they are the beneficiaries of past and present racism, and that the sins of the father may well have been visited on the children.

And yet young whites tell themselves that they had nothing to do with the oppression of black people. They have a stronger belief in their racial innocence than any previous generation of whites, and a natural hostility toward anyone who would challenge that innocence. So (with a great deal of individual variation) they can end up in the paradoxical position of being hostile to blacks as a way of defending their own racial innocence.

I think this is what the young white editors of *The Dartmouth Review* were doing when they shamelessly harassed William Cole, a black music professor. Weren't they saying, in effect, I am so free of racial guilt that I can afford to ruthlessly attack blacks and still be racially innocent? The ruthlessness of that attack was a form of denial, a badge of innocence. The more they were charged with racism, the more ugly and confrontational their harassment became. Racism became a means of rejecting racial guilt, a way of showing that they were not ultimately racists.

The politics of difference sets up a struggle for innocence among all groups. When difference is the currency of power, each group must fight for the innocence that entitles it to power. Blacks sting whites with guilt, remind them of their racist past, accuse them of new and more subtle forms of racism. One way whites retrieve their innocence is to discredit blacks and deny their difficulties, for in this denial is the denial of their own guilt. To blacks this denial looks like racism, a racism that feeds black innocence and encourages them to throw more guilt at whites. And so the cycle continues. The politics of difference leads each group to pick at the sore spots of the other.

Men and women who run universities -- whites, mostly -- also participate in the politics of difference, although they handle their guilt differently than many of their students. They don't deny it, but still they don't want to *feel* it. And to avoid this feeling of guilt they have tended to go along with whatever blacks put on the table rather than work with them to assess their real needs. University administrators have too often been afraid of their own guilt and have relied on negotiation and capitulation more to appease that guilt than to help blacks and other minorities. Administrators would never give white students a racial theme house where they could be "more comfortable with people of their own kind," yet more and more universities are doing this for black students, thus fostering a kind of voluntary segregation. To avoid the anxieties of integrated situations, blacks ask for theme houses; to avoid guilt, white administrators give them theme houses.

When everyone is on the run from his anxieties about race, race relations on campus can be reduced to the negotiation of avoidances. A pattern of demand and concession develops in which each side uses the other to escape itself. Black studies departments, black deans of student affairs, black counseling programs, Afro houses, black theme houses, black homecoming dances and graduation ceremonies -- black students and white administrators have slowly engineered a machinery of separatism that, in the name of sacred difference, redraws the ugly lines of segregation.

Black students have not sufficiently helped themselves, and universities, despite all their concessions, have not really done much for blacks. If both faced their anxieties, I think they would see the same thing: Academic parity with all other groups should be the overriding mission of black students, and it should also be the first goal that universities have for their black students. Blacks can only know they are as good as others when they are, in fact, as good -- when their grades are higher and their dropout rate lower. Nothing under the sun will substitute for this, and no amount of concessions will bring it about.

Universities and colleges can never be free of guilt until they truly help black students, which means leading and challenging them rather than negotiating and capitulating. It means inspiring them to achieve academic parity, nothing less, and helping them see their own weaknesses as their greatest challenge. It also means dismantling the machinery of separatism, breaking the link between difference and power, and skewing the formula for entitlement away from race and gender and back to constitutional rights.

As for the young white students who have rediscovered swastikas and the word "nigger," I think they suffer from an exaggerated sense of their own innocence, as if they were incapable of evil and beyond the reach of guilt. But it is also true that the politics of difference creates an environment which threatens their innocence and makes them defensive. White students are not invited to the negotiating table from which they see blacks and others walk away with concessions. The presumption is that they do not deserve to be there because they are white. So they can only be defensive, and the less mature among them will be aggressive. Guerrilla activity will ensue. Of course this is wrong, but it is also a reflection of an environment where difference carries power and where whites have the wrong "difference."

I think universities should emphasize commonality as a higher value than "diversity" and "pluralism" -- buzzwords for the politics of difference. Difference that does not rest on a clearly delineated foundation of commonality not only is inaccessible to those who are not part of the ethnic or racial group but is antagonistic to them. Difference can enrich only the common ground.

Integration has become an abstract term today, having to do with little more than numbers and racial balances. But it once stood for a high and admirable set of values. It made difference second to commonality, and it asked members of all races to face whatever fears they inspired in each other. I doubt the word will have a new vogue, but the values, under whatever name, are worth working for.

12

On the Scarcity of Black Professors

Abigail Thernstrom

Derrick A. Bell of the Harvard Law School has announced that he will be teaching classes next fall but refusing any pay. Unless, that is, the school appoints a female black to a tenured professorship. The law school now has five black faculty members but all are male. Professor Bell contends that male teachers are role models only for male students. Black women, he declares, need black women teachers.

Jesse Jackson, leading a supportive rally at the law school, has placed Professor Bell in the company of Rosa Parks, Dr. Martin Luther King, Jr., and Nelson Mandela. But no other member of the Harvard faculty, black or white, has joined in what Bell has called his "sacrificial, financial fast." On the other hand, whites are evidently not expected to. Whites, it seems, act and think differently. And blacks who fail to grasp that difference "look black" but "think white." Or at least that is how Professor Bell has described his four black colleagues at the law school -- colleagues who are unwilling "to take risks for what they believe."

Randall Kennedy is among those who look black but allegedly think white. He is on the appointments committee and contends that the law school is making a good-faith effort to find both minority and women faculty. (Nearly half the appointments in the last ten years have been either black or female.) But the particular pool from which the school is drawing its black appointments is very small. Blacks have come to the law schools in large numbers only relatively recently. Moreover, the best and brightest among the black students, with few exceptions, choose to become practicing attor-

On the Scarcity of Black Professorsrs orignally appeared in **Commentary**, July 1990.

neys. A Ph.D. in English is a qualification only for a university job; a top law graduate can earn over $60,000 per annum after only three years at law school -- twice the pay of a starting assistant professor who is likely to have spent at least twice as many years getting a Ph.D. In fact, the prestige and pay of a position in a Wall Street firm are likely to appeal especially to black students, relatively few of whom come from wealthy or socially secure families.

The law school's contention that it is looking but not finding is not accepted by Professor Bell and his allies. In their view it is looking for the wrong sorts of people -- candidates with "upper-class-based qualifications." "Gucci" candidates, another Boston-area law professor has styled them, or candidates with "brand-name" credentials: a J.D. from an elite law school, a clerkship with a federal judge, perhaps a stint at a prestigious firm. "They want people like themselves, or what they wanted to be," Bell has said. The alternative he proposes is more "flexible" criteria.

The drama that is being played out at the Harvard Law School is but one scene in a lengthy play. The larger story involves almost all institutions of higher education in America. Across the nation, universities and colleges are looking hard for minority faculty. An American Council on Education survey, released last summer, indicated that eight out of ten schools were making some sort of effort to hire more minority professors; 30 percent said they were making "a lot" of effort.

To cite only a few examples: in 1988 the University of Wisconsin laid out a five-year plan to increase its minority faculty and academic staff by 75 percent. Duke University has pledged to add one minority faculty member to every department in 1993. By state law, 30 percent of all new faculty in California community colleges must be minority, and, in an effort to meet that goal, the colleges hold "affirmative-action job fairs." Wellesley College has already approved the taking on of five additional minority faculty members over the next five years and is considering a requirement that each department hire a minority-group member when it next makes an appointment. Yale has committed itself to a five-year plan to recruit minority professors and is financially prepared to meet the competition from other schools. Other schools are also reaching deep into their pockets, making extraordinary offers, and suspending normal search processes -- grabbing almost anyone they can find. Minority candidates are often hired even when there has been no advertised job opening. These appointments are called "targets of opportunity."

Some of the schools that have come up with five-year plans and the like are genuinely committed to "diversifying" the faculty. Others are simply deflecting political pressure: protests or threatened protests or task-force reports written to head off potential protests have been behind much of the action. But whatever the motive, the hunt for minority faculty is on -- in great universities and small rural ones alike.

The chances for success, however, are slim. Extravagant goals can be set; they are unlikely to be met. Or rather, they are unlikely to be met unless schools are willing to fill their minority quotas entirely with Asians. The reason is simple: the demand is great and the supply very limited. Thus, where blacks in particular are concerned, even the most prestigious schools are often coming up empty-handed. The Afro-American Studies Department at Harvard, created in 1969, is down to one tenured professor -- and he is white, though not for lack of trying to hire a black. Three offers went out this year to black scholars; none was accepted. And of course Afro-American Studies is not the only department engaged in a search; at least in theory, everyone at Harvard is in on the act. Yet today the number of blacks who are permanent members of the faculty of arts and sciences is smaller than it was in the years 1976 to 1979.

The picture is much the same elsewhere. Take the University of Wisconsin. For it to meet its stated goal, it must not only add 70 minority professors over the next three years; it must also retain those minority faculty members it already has, which will not be easy. Indeed, in the first year of its five-year plan, it added 18 new minority professors but lost even more to other schools.

But where did these institutions expect to find new recruits in such large numbers? In analyzing the problem, it is useful to focus on blacks, since most of the attention has centered on them.

In 1988, according to an authoritative report of the National Academy of Sciences, approximately 16,000 doctoral degrees were awarded to citizens of the United States by American universities. (This figure does not include degrees in education, business administration, and related subjects that are not part of the curriculum of most liberal arts colleges.) This Ph.D. pool is obviously the prime source of new faculty members for our more than 3,000 institutions of higher learning.

How many of the new Ph.D's in 1988 were received by American blacks? If blacks were represented in proportion to their numbers in the population, the figure would be about 2,100 -- or 12 percent. The actual number is less than 400 -- 357 to be precise. Which is to say that a group comprising 12 percent of the population got 2.2 percent of the degrees.

Moreover, here are some (by no means all) of the major research and teaching fields in which there was not a single black Ph.D. in the entire country: astronomy, astrophysics, botany, oceanography, ecology, immunology, demography, geography, European history, classics, comparative literature, and German, Italian, Russian, Chinese, Japanese, and Arabic languages and literature. Then there are the fields where the score is not zero but so close to zero that it might as well be. Of the 608 Americans receiving Ph.D.'s in mathematics or computer science, there were just two blacks. Of the 496 in earth, atmospheric, and marine sciences, there were another two.

Perhaps even more startling than the absence of blacks completing their scholarly training in a science, or in a field involving some remote language or culture, are the figures for the social sciences, where black doctorates are disproportionately concentrated (if we can speak of disproportionate concentration when the numbers involved are so small). Of the 158 black Ph.D.'s in the social sciences, well over half (96) were in the single field of psychology, which left a mere 62 spread thinly through economics, sociology, anthropology, and political science, each of them disciplines of obvious relevance to an understanding of race relations. 1988 yielded a grand total of five new anthropologists, eleven economists, seven political scientists, and fourteen sociologists who were American-born blacks.

What about American history, which of course includes the field of Afro-American history? The total was just five blacks for the entire nation -- fewer than the number of American historians at many relatively small colleges. Students and concerned faculty often argue that schools that really care will at the very minimum employ a black scholar to teach Afro-American history. Where will they find them?

Discouraging as these numbers are, they are getting worse. Between 1978 and 1988 the percentage of degrees awarded to blacks declined by almost a quarter (23 percent). Preliminary figures for 1989 Ph.D.'s have been released by the National Research Council (NRC), and the picture looks much the same as in 1988. "I'd classify the minority situation as a disaster," a member of the NRC staff has remarked.*

Are schools making an insufficient effort to recruit black graduate students? Clearly not. With Mellon Foundation help, 19 colleges and universities are putting in place programs to entice black (and other minority) undergraduates to enter certain Ph.D. programs. The benefits of participation include an offer to repay college loans up to $10,000. From the moment black (and other minority) students arrive at Tulane University they are encouraged in a variety of ways to choose an academic career. At a Pennsylvania conference on graduate school opportunities in February, the 400 minority students in attendance, most of them black, left with the promise of full tuition scholarships if they chose to hire a counselor to assist the students in applying to graduate programs. Harvard rolls out a red carpet for all black and other minority graduate students, providing full financial support, regardless of need. Bill Cosby's children would be eligible for full support.

The pool of potential applicants to graduate schools of arts and sciences is so small in part because academically successful black undergraduates -- like their counterparts in law school -- are not generally interested in an academic career. They go on to more lucrative and prestigious careers. Again, blacks are not more avaricious than whites, but they come from poorer backgrounds. Even when their families have incomes comparable to those of middle-class whites, they do not have comparable assets (the average assets of white families are eleven times those of black families.)

Yet even if the level of interest in graduate education were high, the pool would still be small. For the number of blacks who are graduating from college with successful academic records in relevant fields -- records that suggest they are well-prepared to do graduate work -- is not large.

Perhaps the main reason is -- to put it simply -- that colleges are taking in black students who are not prepared to meet the college's academic demands. And students who do poorly in college are obviously poor candidates for graduate school admission.

As a recent American Council on Education survey found -- confirming what many have sensed simply by looking around -- the vast majority of

* All these numbers would be slightly larger if one were to include West Indians, but many proponents of "diversity" want only American blacks counted. Only they serve as real "role models," these people say.

colleges are attempting to increase the number of minority students on campus. Of the 370 colleges and universities that responded to the survey questionnaire, only 17 percent said they were making no effort to increase the number of minority students, and only 22 percent said they had not expanded financial support for minorities. Such financial aid can be quite extraordinary. Every black freshman who enters Florida Atlanta University next year, for instance, will receive a scholarship that amounts to free tuition for all four years. The school claims that it is doing only what the market demands -- that colleges and universities across the country are recruiting black students with offers of financial assistance.

Many schools have ill-disguised quotas that favor minority candidates. In California there are eight white high school graduates for every black, yet there are only four whites for each black admitted to UCLA or UC Berkeley -- the flagship schools. Black high school graduates are therefore twice as likely as their white classmates to be found at UCLA or Berkeley. And indeed, the black admission rate is double that of whites. That would obviously make sense if the test scores and grades of black applicants were superior to those of whites and Asians. But the opposite is the case. Among California's black high school graduates, only 4.5 percent meet the admission standards of the state's system. Blacks, in fact, have the lowest eligibility rate of any group. At Berkeley, the average 1987 combined SAT score for blacks was 952, which put them (on average) only in the 6th percentile compared to whites and Asians. In other words, 94 percent of Asians and whites got better test scores than the average black freshman.

Schools are not only eagerly enrolling minority students; they are working hard to retain those who come. But the record is not good in this area either. Here are some figures for high school graduates who entered four year institutions in 1980 -- when admission standards for minorities were higher than they are now: while 52 percent of those who were white received bachelor's degrees by 1986, black graduation rates were roughly half of that number. And here are the precise figures for the UC Berkeley class of 1987: while 71 percent of the whites and 67 percent of the Asians received their bachelor's degrees by 1987 or 1988, the rate of completion for blacks was 37 percent (for Hispanics it was 43 percent).

In short, if universities and colleges are having a hard time finding blacks to hire, it is because too few blacks are receiving Ph.D.'s to meet the demand. Not many black students find an academic career enticing, but, equally important, a high percentage of blacks admitted to the colleges from which future Ph.D.'s come are unprepared for the work required, with the consequence that the dropout rates are high.

To be sure, others tell a different story. The pool of black Ph.D.'s may be small, but why, they ask, must professors have a doctorate? In any case, the indictment continues, those institutions of higher education with the most prestige and money -- places like Harvard -- could certainly find people of color if they wanted them. Yet the graduate faculties of arts and sciences -- like the law schools -- are allegedly applying the wrong standards in recruiting and promoting minority faculty. Croliva Herron, an assistant professor in Afro-American Studies at Harvard, has recently complained that the administration there refuses to understand that minority faculty think that writing books is "boring." But if Harvard remains so misguided as to demand evidence of scholarship in the form of (boring) books, other schools are apparently more enlightened. Nine of them offered Professor Herron positions, and she is going to Mount Holyoke with tenure.

As for the low level of black success in college, other explanations abound. Black students are not doing well because, according to a member of the Duke faculty, they must "fight against the prevailing suspicion about their competence." (If true, that would be an argument against affirmative action.) Another frequent suggestion is that they are dropping out because of the "resurgence of bigotry" on campus. A third contention is that, as Reginald Wilson of the American Council of Education puts it, "there's a statistical relation between blacks on campus (i.e., black faculty) and success of black students." Hire more black faculty, and black students will get better grades.

Here we come to the role model argument that lies at the heart of much that is said on the need for "diversity" (and that Professor Bell of the Harvard Law School has simply taken one step further): blacks need blacks, just as women need women. (And Catholics, Catholics? -- they too are in short supply in universities.)

Admittedly, there is a small element of truth here: black students have needed to know that blacks can teach -- that scholarship is not something only whites can do. But that point is certainly well-established by now, and it should not be permitted to obscure a larger one. Role model proponents seem to think of modern education as the equivalent of a medieval apprenticeship. They apparently believe that you attach yourself to a master -- an older version of yourself whom you hope one day to replace -- and learn through a process of identification. They miss the main point about modern and open societies; that they allow people to identify not simply with those who look like them or speak like them but with the universe of humanity.

Role model proponents also miss the point that books are the keys which open the doors to that larger world. Our sense of ourselves and our understanding of the world can and does expand in encounters with writers -- and teachers -- with whom we seem to share little. They may look different and speak in a different tongue; we may even suspect that we would not like them, were we to be introduced. But good books fashion bonds among seemingly dissimilar people, and surely one role of the teacher is to help the student gain access to such books.

There is also much talk about the need for more role models in our elementary and high schools, where the poor performance of so many black children naturally affects the size of the pool of college-bound seniors, as well as of those who go on to good graduate schools and from whose ranks minority scholars must be drawn.

Nationwide, half of all black children attend school in an inner-city district. Take Boston, which is pretty typical of inner-city school systems. In Boston, four out of ten students drop out before the twelfth grade; particularly high are the drop-out rates for black males. This year, an estimated 40 percent of the seniors were not expected to pass an eighth grade reading test that had been made a graduation requirement. The school committee cancelled the test.

In the last six years, Boston has bought new textbooks, instituted new programs, and added dozens of teachers, many of them black. Still, there has been virtually no improvement in reading or math achievement scores since 1984. In almost half the elementary schools in the city, all but four of the middle schools, and all but one of the non-exam high schools, students scores rank among the lowest 25 percent in the state. Thus, almost a third of the sixth-graders who took a basic reading test in 1986-87 failed it (or else either could not complete it or did not take it during the three-week period in which they had a chance to do so). Furthermore, black scores are significantly worse than white, and the gap between the two groups is growing. In 1984 white students scored between 12 and 20 percentile points better than black students in all grades in reading. In 1988 the gap widened to between 17 and 25 points.

At the college level, too, there is much in the way of "reform." In California, such a high percentage of black and other minority students in the state colleges and universities are failing to graduate that there is talk of moving into what we might call a second stage of affirmative action. To this end a bill, authored by Tom Hayden of '60s fame, has been passed in the California State Assembly -- and is now under consideration in the Senate -- that would institute a two-track system of student admissions, one based on merit and the other explicitly on race and ethnicity. And although the bill's language is somewhat ambiguous, it seems to ensure for that second track not only admission but academic success -- equal graduation rates.

In addition to addressing the question of minority student representation (in the freshman and graduating classes), the Hayden bill also concerns itself with faculty quality. On the assumption that drop out rates reflect a university atmosphere hostile to minority aspirations, the bill stipulates that all segments of public higher education in the state would "be expected to establish programs to promote racial and cultural sensitivity and understanding in instructional and counseling programs, including the consideration of efforts to promote this sensitivity and understanding in the evaluation of faculty and other instructional staff ..."

But if, in the hiring and promotion of faculty, evidence of an effort to promote "racial sensitivity" would have to be taken into account, the Hayden bill does not specify what would constitute insufficient effort on this front. Can whites ever meet the requisite standard of sensitivity and understanding? What about those black scholars who "think white"?

The direction in which California may be heading is not unique. The Middle States Association of Colleges and Schools, which is an accrediting agency, now defers certification if a school fails to measure up in terms of minority faculty recruitment, minority student retention, and racial atmosphere. Too many minority drop-outs, too few blacks on the faculty, too much racial tension, and (as Baruch College in New York has discovered) the school will have its accreditation put on hold. In many schools the process of internal monitoring is enough to keep the pressure up. Affirmative action officers often have the power to scrutinize closely all proposed appointments. In fact, such personnel are now sitting in on job interviews, questioning candidates for a position in history, say, with an eye to their views on racial matters.

The truth is that none of these measures will touch the core of the problem: the poor academic performance of black students at every level. And only when that picture changes will the size of the pool of black Ph.D.'s greatly enlarge.

Nevertheless, all is far from hopeless. In part, change will have to come from blacks themselves. For instance, too many black students think of good grades as "white" -- a problem that blacks themselves are beginning to talk about. But institutions of higher education can themselves play a constructive role -- not, however, by justifying policies that amount to an acceptance of a racial double standard; and not by changing the curriculum, grading faculty on a racial-sensitivity scale, establishing sensitivity workshops, or fashioning racial harassment codes. These only debase scholarly standards, promote censorship and self-censorship, and trigger white resentment.

What universities and colleges *can* do -- and what some are already doing -- is to get involved in education at the level at which it really counts for black students. This means linking up with high schools, tutoring inner-city students, and running special summer programs.

Perhaps the most exciting such program is the one being put in place in Chelsea, Massachusetts, by Boston University. The university has been invited to manage the public school system for an experimental ten years, and it plans not only to alter the learning and teaching environment in the schools themselves but also in the home. The program includes adult literacy training, seminars on parenting, classes for teenage mothers to teach life-coping skills, and pre-natal health care -- all of which will help students come to school ready to learn. In sharp contrast to gestures like Derrick Bell's, the efforts of Boston University and other such institutions are rays of hope in a largely bleak scene.

13

The Supreme Court's "Second Thoughts" About Race and the Constitution

Henry Mark Holzer

Beginning with President Reagan's appointment of Sandra Day O'Connor to the Supreme Court, I and many others hoped that new appointees would at least attempt to thwart the Liberals' agenda generally and their racial programs particularly. We have been disappointed more than once, and two cases last year raised serious doubts about the Court's willingness and/or its ability to stop Liberal racial policies. Those policies have been high on the Liberal agenda, especially in the post-World War II years, and for a long time Liberals have had their own way. I refer not to their legitimate goals, which all Americans should have shared -- ending racial segregation in public schools and other government-operated institutions, securing voting rights for the disenfranchised, removing apartheid-like bars to interracial marriage -- but rather to their advancing of two indefensible notions on the subject of race, notions on which even the Reagan-Rehnquist Court appear to be perpetuating into the Twenty-First Century America.

The first of the Liberals' high-agenda racial notions is that government should possess the power to prevent private racial discrimination. The second is that government itself should possess the power to discriminate not against racial minorities, but on their behalf.

Although the first Supreme Court acceptance of the notion that private racial discrimination was unconstitutional came in the 1948 case of *Shelley v. Kraemer* -- holding that racially restrictive land covenants, though valid, were unconstitutional if enforced in court -- the idea really took hold with enactment of the Civil Rights Act of 1964 and the decision of two cases interpreting it.

The Heart of Atlanta Motel in Georgia and Ollie's Barbecue, an Alabama restaurant, had inflexible policies against accommodating Negroes. The owners of the establishments decided that since the business belonged to them, they would serve whomever they pleased.

Needless to say, to a great many people in the United States, racial discrimination had always -- rightly -- been anathema, both on the governmental level, where one found legislation like the South's Jim Crow laws, and in the private sector, where it was not uncommon to encounter attitudes like those of the Heart of Atlanta Motel and Ollie's Barbecue. Following World War II, however, gains began to be made against official state and local racial discrimination, and the Supreme Court's landmark public school desegregation case was probably the most striking example from the decade after the War.[1]

The cutting edge in those days in the fight against official, government racial discrimination was the Fourteenth Amendment to the Constitution of the United States, which provides that: " ...nor shall any State deprive any person of life, liberty, or property without due process of law; nor deny to any person within its jurisdiction the equal protection of the laws."[2] But for Liberals, it was not enough to attack merely *public* racial discrimination. They also insisted on reaching the *private* discrimination practiced by all the Heart of Atlanta Motels and Ollie's Barbecues of this country.

This public/private distinction is one that must be carefully understood, especially in regard to racial discrimination. It is axiomatic that government -- state and federal -- must not discriminate racially. Indeed, the Constitution expressly prohibits *public* racial discrimination.

On the other hand, as irrational and immoral as private racial discrimination is -- treating an entire race as an undifferentiated collective whole -- the Constitution nowhere bars it. No more than it bars marrying elderly spinsters for their money, parental indifference to the spiritual needs of their children, or religious bigotry. Indeed, the very nature of a free country and of its Constitution necessarily distinguishes between public and private morality.

---

[1] Brown v. Board of Education, 347 U.S. 483 (1954).
[2] Emphasis added.

As much as victims of racial discrimination had a *constitutional* right to nondiscriminatory treatment by government, and a *moral* right to it by other *individuals*, these were two entirely separate kinds of rights. To attempt to combine the two or to erase the differences, to assert that the Constitution required private individuals to eschew racial prejudice was, in effect, to make government the arbiter of private morality. It was also to eliminate the difference between public and private conduct, to compel some people to fulfill the aspirations of others (however legitimate), and, in so doing, to ignore the fact that no one can have their supposed "rights" vindicated by violating the actual rights of others. But none of these points, or any others, prevented the Liberals from attempting to convert their constituents' moral rights into constitutional ones.

Since the Liberals could not use the Fourteenth Amendment for that purpose -- because of its requirement that the discriminatory action be taken by the State -- they went shopping elsewhere. As a result, in the early '60s a broad-based federal Civil Rights Act was proposed, designed to rest on an entirely different base from the Fourteenth Amendment. One part of the Act was intended to reach private racially discriminatory conduct in a host of so called "public accommodations."

Though the proposed legislation had a great many Congressional supporters, some of them, as well as others in the legislature, had serious reservations about whether Congress could reach the private racially discriminatory practices of local business establishments. The Senate Hearings in 1963 spotlighted the problem:[3]

Attorney General Kennedy: We base this on the commerce clause.

Senator Moroney: ...many of us are worried about the use the interstate commerce clause will have on matters which have been for more than 170 years thought to be within the realm of local control under our dual system of State and Federal government.

* * *

Senator Moroney: I strongly doubt that we can stretch the interstate commerce clause that far....

* * *

Senator Moroney: If the court decisions . . . mean that a business, no matter how intrastate in its nature, comes under the interstate commerce clause, then we canlegislate for other businesses in other fields in addition to the discrimination legislation that is asked for here.

---

[3] See Hearings Before the Senate Committee on Commerce on S.1732, 88th Cong., 1st Sess., parts 1 and 2.

> **Attorney General Kennedy:** If the establishment is covered by the commerce clause, then you can regulate; that is correct ..
>
> **Senator Thurmond:** Mr. Attorney General, isn't it true that all of the acts of Congress based on the commerce clause . . . were primarily designed to regulate economic affairs of life and that the basic purpose of this bill is to regulate moral and social affairs.
>
> **Attorney General Kennedy:** . . . I think that the discrimination that is taking place at the present time is having a very adverse effect on our economy.

Members of Congress were not the only ones deeply concerned about extending federal interstate commerce power so as to control local business establishments. One of America's most distinguished constitutional law authorities, Professor Gerald Gunther, unequivocally informed the Department of Justice that use of the interstate commerce clause to bar private racial discrimination in local places of "public accommodation" would be unconstitutional:

> The commerce clause "hook" has been put to some rather strained uses in the past, I know; but the substantive content of the commerce clause would have to be drained beyond any point yet reached to justify the simplistic argument that all intrastate activity may be subjected to any kind of national regulation merely because some formal crossing of an interstate boundary once took place....The aim of the proposed anti-discrimination legislation, I take it, is quite unrelated to any concern with

It would, I think, pervert the meaning and purpose of the commerce clause to invoke it as the basis for this legislation.

It should be noted that neither the Senators quoted above nor Professor Gunther objected to the Civil Rights Act per se and the effect it would have on private racial discrimination in local business establishments. Indeed, they welcomed both. Their opposition was limited solely to the constitutional base the legislation would rest on, preferring, not the commerce clause, but the Fourteenth Amendment. But the Civil Rights Act of 1964 was enacted anyhow, predicated on Congress's interstate commerce power.[5] Before the end of that year, the constitutionality of its "public accommodations" provisions was before the Supreme Court in the *Heart of Atlanta*[6] and *Ollie's Barbecue*[7] cases.

---

4 See Gerald Gunther, Constitutional Law Cases and Materials, 10th ed., (The Foundation Press, 1980), p. 203

5 78 Stat. 241-268

6 Heart of Atlanta Motel, Inc. v. United States, 379 U.S. 241 (1964).

7 Katzenbach v. McClung, 379 U.S. 294 (1964)

The question for the Court in each case was the same: did Congress exceed its constitutional powers under the interstate commerce clause in compelling the owners of local, privately owned businesses to serve customers whom they declined to serve for racially motivated reasons?

The answer was a unanimous, resounding "no."

To reach that result, the Court relied on earlier cases in which it had allowed Congress to regulate such aspects of business as the sale of products, wages and hours, labor relations, crop control, pricing, and more, because those aspects had some connection with interstate commerce. These precedents, together with the motel's and restaurant's tenuous relationship with interstate commerce through the former's guests and the latter's food purchases, were deemed sufficient by the Court to allow Congress to impose the public accommodations provisions of the federal Civil Rights Act on the two local businesses. That conclusion was undesirable for two reasons: first, as an unwarranted extension of the interstate commerce clause which, by 1964, was an old story anyhow; and second, and much more important, as the conversion of legitimate private aspirations into legal entitlement and reprehensible private behavior into unconstitutional conduct.

The Liberals had won, translating their view of racial morality into constitutionally-rooted public policy. After all, that had really caused the enactment of the federal Civil Rights Act of 1964? The Senate Hearings quoted above provide the revealing answer:

> **Attorney General Kennedy:** Senator, I think that there is an injustice that needs to be remedied. We have to find the tools with which to remedy that injustice....
>
> * * *
>
> **Senator Cooper:** I do not suppose that anyone would seriously contend that the administration is proposing legislation, or the Congress is considering legislation, because it has suddenly determined, after all these years,that segregation is a burden on interstate commerce. We are considering legislation because we believe, as the great majority of people in our country believe, that all citizens have an equal right to have access to goods, services, and facilities which are held out to be available for public use and patronage.
>
> * * *
>
> **Senator Pastore:** I believe in this bill because I believe in the dignity of man, not because it impedes our commerce. I don't think any man has the right to say to another man, you can't eat in my restaurant because you have a dark skin; no matter how clean you are, you can't eat in my restaurant. That deprives a man of his full stature as an American citizen. That shocks me. That hurts me. And that is the reason why I want to vote for this law

> Now it might well be that I can effect the same remedy through the commerce clause. But I like to feel that what we are talking about is a moral issue, an issue that involves the morality of this great country of ours.[8]

In the same vein, the Report of the Senate Commerce Committee and candidly admitted that:

> The primary purpose of . . . [the Civil Rights Act], then, is to solve this problem, the deprivation of personal dignity that surely accompanies denials of equal access to public [sic] establishments. Discrimination is not simply dollars and cents, hamburgers and movies; it is the humiliation, frustration and embarrassment that a person must surely feel when he is told that he is unacceptable also a member of the public because of his race or color.[9]

In sum, as Justice Arthur J. Goldberg so clearly admitted when concurring in *Heart of Atlanta* and *Katzenbach*: "The primary purpose of the Civil Rights Act of 1964, however, as the Court recognizes, and as I would underscore, is the *vindication of human dignity* and not mere economics."[10] However, to "vindicate" that human dignity, Congress and the Court (especially the Court) had seen to it that the fundamental distinction between public and private conduct, embodied in the Constitution generally and in the Fourteenth Amendment's "state action" requirement in particular, as virtually erased. The situation worsened with the Court's decision in *Jones v. Alfred H. Mayer Co.*[11] four years later.[12]

Following the Civil War, Congress enacted the Civil Rights Act of 1866. One of its provisions evolved into the following federal statute: "All citizens of the United States shall have the same right, in every State and Territory, as is enjoyed by white citizens thereof to inherit, purchase, lease, sell, hold and convey real and personal property."

When in the mid-1960s, a white developer in St. Louis refused to sell a house to a Negro named Jones, he sued under Section 1982. Although it had long been the law -- rightly -- that government could not discriminatorily deny any American the right to buy or rent property because of race or color, neither Section 1982 nor any other provision of law had ever been held applicable to purely *private* racial discrimination in housing. So the question

---

[8] Hearings Before the Senate Committee on Commerce on S.1732, 88th Cong., 1st Sess., part 1 and 2; emphasis added.
[9] Senate Report No. 872, 88th Congress, 2d Sess. 16.
[10] Heart of Atlanta Motel, Inc. v. United States, 379 U.S. 241 (1964).
[11] 392 U.S. 409 (1968).
[12] 42 U.S.C. 1982.

that the Supreme Court eventually had to decide in *Jones v. Alfred H. Mayer Co.* was obviously an important one.

In a 7-2 opinion written by Justice Stewart, which relied very heavily on the majority's perception of the original intent of Congress when it enacted the statute, the Court held that Section 1982 prohibited "all discrimination against Negroes in the sale or rental of property -- discrimination by private owners as well as discrimination by public authorities."[13]

The Court's conclusion also rested in part on the Thirteenth Amendment, which had abolished slavery. Justice Stewart wrote that:

> Negro citizens, North and South, who saw in the Thirteenth Amendment a promise of freedom -- freedom to "go and come at pleasure" [footnote omitted] and to "buy and sell when they please" [footnote omitted] -- would be left with "a mere paper guarantee" [footnote omitted] if Congress were powerless to assure that a dollar in the hands of a Negro will purchase the same thing as a dollar in the hands of a white man. At the very least, the freedom that Congress is empowered to secure under the Thirteenth Amendment includes the freedom to buy whatever a white man can buy, the right to live wherever a white man can live.[14]

There were two major flaws in the majority opinion. One, ably dealt with in Justice Harlan's dissent (joined by Justice White) as that neither the language of the statute itself, nor the congressional intent on which the majority had predicated its interpretation of the statute, was nearly so supportive of the majority's conclusion as Justice Stewart has contended. Justice Harlan put the point nicely when he noted that:

> [My] analysis of the language, structure, and legislative history of the 1866 Civil Rights Act shows, I believe, that the Court's thesis that the Act was meant to extend to purely private action is open to the most serious doubt, if indeed it does not render that thesis wholly untenable. Another, albeit less tangible, consideration points in the same direction. Many of the legislators who took part in the congressional debates inevitably must have shared the individualistic ethic of their time, which emphasized personal freedom [footnote omitted] and embodied a distaste for governmental interference which was soon to culminate in the era of laissez-faire [footnote omitted]. It seems to me that most of these men would have regarded it as a great intrusion on individual liberty for the government to take from a man the power to refuse for personal reasons to enter into a purely private transaction involving the disposition of property, albeit those personal reasons might reflect racial bias.[15]

---

[13] Jones v. Alfred H. Mayer Co., 392 U.S. 409, 421, 88 S.Ct. 2186, 2194 (1968).
[14] 392 U.S. at 473-474.
[15] Ibid.

Interestingly, although Harlan's analysis led him to disagree with the majority's *conclusion*, he did not disagree with the majority's basic premise that purely *private* racial discrimination could be prohibited by government power. Indeed, between the time of oral argument in *Jones* in April 1968 and the case's decision in June 1968, Congress had enacted the Civil Rights Act of 1968, containing comprehensive "fair housing" provisions dealing with the refusal to sell real property for racial reasons. Harlan considered the entire new Civil Rights Act "presumptively constitutional."[16]

The other major flaw in the majority's approach was a failure adequately to distinguish between the nature and significance of private versus *government* action.[17] A concurring opinion by Justice Douglas inadvertently highlighted that failure. As usual, he was eloquent but overbroad, glossing over the crucial distinction on which the case, and the principle behind it, rested. Douglas correctly observed that, unfortunately: "Some badges of slavery remain today. While the institution has been outlawed, it has remained in the minds and hearts of many white men. Cases that have come to this Court depict a spectacle of slavery unwilling to die."[18] Then, he listed examples. Without distinguishing between government and private action, he threw into the same undifferentiated pot racially segregated *public* schools, and racially discriminatory *private* restaurants; *state* laws against racial intermarriage, and *personal* racial preferences in renting motel rooms; *municipal* ordinances establishing residential districts according to race, and *individual* refusals to sell real estate because of racial prejudice.

Douglas's refusal to distinguish between private and government discrimination; and the majority's mistaken willingness to believe that the 1866 Congress intended to prohibit even *private* racial discrimination in the transfer of real property; and Harlan's disagreement only with the interpretation of the legislative history, but not with the principle that government can bar private racial discrimination in housing; and, finally, enactment of the Civil Rights Act of 1968 with its Fair Housing Title,[19] all compel the conclusion that since a property owner cannot refuse to sell because of racially discriminatory motives, the line between properly prohibited

---

[16] 392 U.S. at 478. Although Harlan did discuss that difference in his analysis of the statute's legislative history, he failed to assess its significance.
[17] 392 U.S. at 445.
[18] Ibid.
[19] Title VIII; See Pub. L. 90-284, 82 Stat. 81.

government racial discrimination and improperly prohibited *private* racial discrimination has ceased to be meaningful.

As if to dispel any lingering doubt about its view that federal statutes could bar *private* racial discrimination, the court later reiterated the point. Certain Virginia private schools discriminated racially among applicants, declining to accept Negroes. Children who were excluded, sued. They invoked both the public accommodations sections of the Civil Rights Act of 1964, which had been upheld in *Heart of Atlanta* and *Katzenbach* a decade earlier, and also another, older federal civil rights statute, an analog to Section 1981, which had been before the Court in the *Jones* case. Apparently deciding that the local private schools were measurably different from a motel and a restaurant, the children's attorneys withdrew their public accommodations claim before trial, relying only on the older statute, Title 42 U.S.C. Section 1981, which provides that:

> All persons within the jurisdiction of the United States shall have the same right in every State and Territory to make and enforce contracts, to sue, be parties, give evidence, and to the full and equal benefit of all laws and proceedings for the security of persons and property as is enjoyed by white citizens....

Based on this civil rights statute, the unsuccessful applicants argued that the private schools could not refuse to make contracts with them solely because they were Negroes. The Supreme Court agreed, holding that Section 1981 did reach purely *private* racial discrimination and that it prohibited *all* racially motivated contract decisions.[20] The implications of the *Runyon* decision were, of course, so obvious that two of the majority justices felt obliged virtually to admit that what they were deciding was wrong, and then to explain why they were going along with the majority anyhow.

Justice Powell frankly admitted that "[if] the slate were clean I might well be inclined to agree with [the dissent] that Section 1981 was not intended [by the Congress that enacted it in the post-Civil War period] to restrict private contractual choices.[21]

Why the slate was not clean was explained by the other separately concurring justice, John Stevens: not long before, the Court had ruled on some cases which, though perhaps wrongly decided, compelled the result

---

[20] Runyon v. McCrary, 427 U.S. 160 (1976).
[21] 427 U.S. at 186.

that the majority had reached in *Runyon*. Although Stevens cogently stated why the majority was dead wrong, he went along with it anyhow. He expressed his willingness quite straightforwardly: even if a century earlier Section 1981 had not been intended by its framers to mean what the *Runyon* majority now interpreted it to mean, no matter, because "it surely accords with the prevailing sense of justice today."[22] Justice Stevens was obviously making two fascinating admissions: on the one hand, he entertained grave reservations about allowing federal civil rights legislation to control the myriad contractual aspects of an individual's *private* business relations; but on the other, he was willing to go along because the country's mood (and/or his own) was less concerned with the right of private individuals to run their own lives and businesses their own way, than with the legitimate aspirations of Negroes to enter the American mainstream, even if doing so meant that the government would have to prohibit certain private choices.

Since *Heart of Atlanta* and *Katzenbach* meant that the owner of any business deemed to be a "public accommodation" had no right to serve only those customers he or she chose; since *Jones* meant that there was no private right of racial discrimination concerning the sale of property; since *Runyon* meant that no business could make a racially motivated contract decision; and since all this added up to a pro-minority government posture, speculation about what the Court would do if a state or Congress went so far as actually to impose some sort of a pro-minority racial quota.

Two years after *Runyon*, the court faced a case embodying the second of the Liberals' high-agenda notions on the subject of race: government power used to discriminate not against racial minorities, but *on their behalf*. In other words, quotas.

The court's decision in *Regents of the University of California v. Bakke*[23] was about as fragmented as a Supreme Court decision could be,[24] and also somewhat of a compromise. The Supreme Court recognized that the school's "special admissions program is undeniably a classification based on race and ethnic background. To the extent that there existed a pool of

---

[22] 427 U.S. at 191.
[23] 438 U.S. 265 (1978).
[24] Justice Powell wrote for the "majority" affirming in part and reversing in part. Justices Brennan, White, Marshall, and Blackmun concurred in part and dissented in part. Justices White, Marshall, and Blackmun each filed separate opinions. Justice Stevens concurred in part and dissented in part, and filed an opinion joined by Chief Justice Burger and Justices Stewart and Rehnquist.

at least minimally qualified minority applicants to fill the 16 special admissions seats, white applicants could compete only for 84 seats in the entering class, rather than the 100 open to minority applicants. Whether this limitation is described as a quota or a goal, it is a line drawn on the basis of race and ethnic status."[25]

As such, the plurality opinion held that the University of California's quota was not per se unconstitutional, but only that "when a State's distribution of benefits or imposition of burdens hinges on ancestry or the color of a person's skin, that individual is entitled to a demonstration that the challenged classification is necessary to promote a substantial state interest. [The University of California] has failed to carry this burden."[26] In other words, an important enough government interest *could* sustain a pro-minority racial quota. Two years later the court would face just that situation.

The year before *Bakke* was decided by the Supreme Court, Congress had enacted the Public Works Employment Act of 1977[27] authorizing some $4 billion in federal grants to state and local governments for use in public works projects. There was nothing unusual about that. But one section of the Act[28] was extremely unusual. The "minority business enterprise" provision required that at least 10 percent of each grant go to contractors who were members of statutorily defined minorities: "Negroes, Spanish speaking, Orientals, Indians, Eskimos, and Aleuts."

Despite America's unfortunate experience with government racial classifications; despite constitutional requirements that government be color-blind; despite consistent judicial lip-service to the proposition that racial equality was a two-way street protecting our Caucasian majority as well as our various minorities; and despite the Public Works Employment Act's unequivocal intent to aid certain minorities and to disadvantage non-minorities solely for racial reasons, a divided Supreme Court upheld the minority business enterprise provision of the Act.

The fact that Congress had enacted and the Court had upheld a provision regulating the flow of sizable public works funds to the construction industry on a strictly racial quota basis is not nearly as important as why it did so. For the answer, the place to begin is in Congress.

[25] 438 U.S. at 289.
[26] 438 U.S. at 320.
[27] P.L. 95-28, 91 Stat. 116.
[28] 103 (f) 2.

The provision's sponsor had conceded that its objective was to direct funds into the minority business community[29] and "to begin to redress this grievance that has been extant for so long."[30] Another Congressman viewed the provision as promoting "economic equality" and countering a perpetuation of "the historic practices that have precluded minority businesses from effective participation in public contracting opportunities."[31] These attitudes were representative of the thinking of other Members of Congress, though not all, and of the philosophy of earlier business-related programs that had been concerned with helping "racially disadvantaged" businesses.

When the minority business enterprise provision reached the Supreme Court, the question to be decided was whether Congress could constitutionally favor some businesses and disfavor others *solely* on the basis of racial and ethnic criteria.

The answer was "yes," though, as in *Bakke* two years before, the Court was badly fragmented: Chief Justice Burger and Justices White and Powell joined in one opinion, Powell wrote one of his own, and Justices Marshall, Brennan and Blackmun joined in yet another, to make the six-man majority; the dissents consisted of an opinion by Justice Stewart for himself and Justice Rehnquist, and an opinion by Justice Stevens.

Burger's approach was largely to defer to Congress's concern for the problem of past racial discrimination generally, and minority participation in government-funded construction projects in particular. He observed that:

> Congress, after due consideration, perceived a pressing need to move forward with new approaches in the continuing effort to achieve the goal of equality of economic opportunity. In this effort, Congress has necessary latitude to try new techniques such as the limited use of racial and ethnic criteria to accomplish remedial objectives....That the program may press the outer limits of congressional authority affords no base for striking it down.[32]

Burger's passing reference to "remedial objectives" was enlarged somewhat by Powell, who observed that "in our quest to achieve a society free from racial classification, we cannot ignore the claims of those who still

---

[29] 123 Cong. Rec. H.1388-1389 (Feb. 23, 1977).
[30] 123 Cong. Rec. H1440 (Feb. 24, 1977); emphasis added.
[31] 123 Cong. Rec. H1441 (Feb.24, 1977).
[32] Fullilove v. Klutznick, 448 U.S. 453, 490 (1980); emphasis added.

suffer from the effects of identifiable discrimination."[33] But it was Marshall who named explicitly what all six majority justices were really getting at:

> In my separate opinion in Bakke . . . I recounted the "ingenious and pervasive forms of discrimination against the Negro" long condoned under the Constitution and concluded that "[t]he position of the Negro today in America is the tragic but inevitable consequence of centuries of unequal treatment." I there stated:
>
> It is because of a legacy of unequal treatment that we now must permit the institutions of this society to give consideration to race in making decisions about who will hold the position of influence, affluence, and prestige in America. For far too long, the doors to those positions have been shut to Negroes. If we are ever to become a fully integrated society, one in which the color of a person's skin will not determine the opportunities available to him or her, we must be willing to open those doors...Those doors cannot be fully opened without the acceptance of race-conscious remedies. As my Brother Blackmun observed in Bakke,' [i]n order to get beyond racism, we must first take account of race. There is no other way'...."

Congress recognized these realities when it enacted the minority set-aside provision at issue in this case. Today, by upholding this race-conscious remedy, the Court accords Congress the authority necessary to undertake the task of moving our society toward a state of meaningful equality of opportunity, not an abstract version of equality in which the effects of past discrimination would be forever frozen into our social fabric. I applaud this result.[34]

So, according to the *Fullilove* majority at least, and in a federal rather than a state setting, two wrongs apparently did make a right.

When *Heart of Atlanta*, *Katzenbach*, *Jones*, *Runyon*, and *Fullilove* were decided, the High Court battles of the so-called Reagan Revolution had not yet begun. Sandra Day O'Connor was yet to be appointed, as was Antonin Scalia. Judge Bork's nomination was years in the distance. Anthony M. Kennedy would not become a justice until 1988. But once O'Connor, Scalia, and Kennedy were on board and Associate Justice William H. Rehnquist had replaced Warren Burger as chief, many of us hoped (indeed, expected) that the new "conservative" court would turn away from earlier decisions that had well nigh erased the distinction between public and private discrimination, and had actually approved, in principle and in fact, racial quotas.

In two cases decided last year, the Liberals thought, at least judging by their response, that the court had done just that. For

---

[33] Fullilove v. Klutznick, 448 U.S. 453, 516 (1980).
[34] 448 U.S. at 522.

example, on 12 February 1990 *The New York Times* lamented that the Rehnquist-Reagan Court was guilty of "misreading basic civil rights law" and "persistently crabbed construction."

Unfortunately, the *Times* was correct about the court's dismal performance, but not for the reasons that the newspaper advanced.[35]

One of the two cases is *Patterson v. McLean Credit Union.*[36] It involved Section 1981 of the Civil Rights Act, the same section that had been held in *Runyon* to prohibit racial discrimination in private contracts. Thus, not only did *Patterson* present an opportunity for the court to revisit *Runyon*, but after *Patterson* had been argued, the parties were expressly directed "to brief and argue an additional question: Whether or not the interpretation of [section] 1981 adopted by this court in *Runyon* . . . should be reconsidered.[37]

Although the court would take flak from Liberals for the narrowness of its decision that, as a matter of statutory construction, "racial harassment relating to the conditions of employment is not actionable under Section 1981 because that provision does not apply to conduct which occurs after the formation of a contract and which does not interfere with the right to enforce established contract violations,"[38] Liberals rejoiced when the court announced that: "[We] now decline to overrule our decision in *Runyon*."[39]

Why did the Supreme Court -- Kennedy, O'Connor, Scalia, and Rehnquist, included -- expressly ratify *Runyon*?

Stare decisis. Said Kennedy: "Whether *Runyon*'s interpretation of Section 1981 as prohibiting racial discrimination in the making of private contracts is right or wrong [!] as an original matter, it is certain that it is not inconsistent with the prevailing sense of justice in this country. To the contrary, *Runyon* is entirely consistent with our society's deep commitment to the eradication of discrimination based on a person's race or the color of his skin."[40] As in *Fullilove*, two wrongs apparently still made a right.

*Runyo*n and its tortured (and almost admittedly erroneous, though popular) interpretation of Section 1981 was not the only Liberal-cherished

---

[35] One of the cases is comparatively unimportant. In Martin v. Wilks, 109 S.Ct. 2180 (1989), interpreting common law principles and Federal Rules of Civil Procedure, the court rather unremarkably ruled that non-participants in prior employment discrimination proceedings could challenge decisions made pursuant to consent decrees entered in those proceedings.

[36] 109 S.Ct. at 2363 (1989).

[37] 109 S.Ct. at 2363.

[38] 109 S.Ct. at 2369. But Title VII of the Civil Rights Act of 1964, the court held, does prohibit such harassment.

[39] 109 S.Ct. at 2369.

[40] 109 S.Ct. at 2371.

civil rights issue on the court's docket last year. There was also an opportunity for the now allegedly more conservative court to nail the quotas which sometimes are euphemistically labeled "minority set-asides." In other words, the principle of *Fullilove* was to be revisited.

Richmond, Virginia, required non-minority construction contractors working for that city to subcontract at least 30 percent of the contract's dollar amount to "Minority Business Enterprises."[41] Characterizing Richmond's scheme as "a rigid racial quota in the awarding of public contracts,"[42] Justice O'Connor's opinion for the court struck down the minority set-aside -- but not because quotas are per se unconstitutional, and not because they racially discriminate on behalf of certain minorities. No. The reason was that Richmond did not have a good enough excuse -- such as remedying specific past discrimination. So *Fullilove* stands, and state/local pro-minority racial quotas survive if the "program is narrowly tailored to remedy the effects of prior discrimination,"[43] whatever that means.[44]

Thanks to the Reagan-Rehnquist Court, the net result, then, of *Patterson* and *Croson* is a plus for Liberals. Much, if not most, private racial discrimination is still illegal. *Runyon* lives. Pro-minority quotas are not per se unconstitutional, and in principle can even be valid. *Fullilove* lives.

But why? Because so-called conservative judges are, at root, no different from those of the Liberal left. All of them believe in government power at the expense of individual rights. They disagree only about how the government ought to intervene in people's lives, not whether interference is permissible. Hence, the Liberals destroy private choice in racial matters, and enlist government muscle in behalf of the Left's minority constituencies. The Conservatives' response is, typically, that, well. . . maybe private racial discrimination is really not unconstitutional but everyone wants it to be, and, well . . . maybe racial quotas are not really valid -- unless, of course, the government has a very fine reason. With friends like this....

---

[41] This was defined as 51% ownership and control by U.S. citizens who are "Blacks, Spanish-speaking [!], Oriental, Indians, Eskimos, or Aleuts." (City of Richmond v. J.A. Croson, 109 S.Ct. 706, 713 (1989).

[42] 109 S.Ct. at 724.

[43] 109 S.Ct. at 729.

[44] The final Supreme Court case, Wards Cove Packing Co., Inc. 109 S.Ct. 2115 (1989) -- a 5-4 decision addressing the narrow question of the role of statistical proof in making a prima facie case in a "disparate impact" Title VII employment discrimination action -- is unremarkable, despite the attention the case has received, except for the court's dictum that "a subjective quota system of employment selection" would be "far from the intent of Title VII." (109 S.Ct. at 2122).

What is the answer? There is only one.

Those who would be free -- in matters of racial choice and everything else -- must uncompromisingly stand for individual rights, even if that means allowing people to make choices someone else considers rotten.

No one ever became free by enslaving someone else.

Part IV

The New Racism and the American Dream

David Horowitz

William Allen

14

The Radical Paradigm and the New Racism

David Horowitz

After the hightide of the Civil Rights Revolution of the 1960s had ebbed, a group of black radicals led by James Foreman demanded $400 million in reparations for the 400 years of slavery that African Americans had suffered in this country. Years later, the black economist Thomas Sowell countered this argument by citing the gains that black Americans had made since their arrival from Africa and comparing their current status and economic condition with the terrible plight of their countrymen who had been left behind. Without attempting to diminish the horrors of slavery or of the crime that had brought blacks to America against their will, Sowell suggested that if payments were in order for the consequences of the forced migration it would make as much sense to demand them from blacks themselves for the opportunities they acquired by having been brought here. These conflicting visions provide a good introduction to the paradox of race relations in America today.

It is 25 years since the Civil Rights Revolution and more than a century since the Civil War, yet Americans are still being harrangued about their racial guilt over slavery and segregation, as though neither event had ever taken place. Race, Americans are constantly reminded, is the gravest problem they face as a nation and the heaviest burden of their democratic history.

Charges of "racism" were a central theme in the last presidential election, provoked by the famous TV spots about Willie Horton and liberal myopia on the subject of crime. Suspicions of racism are now key components of all hearings on Supreme Court appointments, with liberal Senators interrogating nominees about their views on poll taxes, voter literacy tests, and the 14th Amendment, as though these issues had not been decided decades before. Editorial writers in the prestige press constantly warn Americans that they must support government programs to redress the outstanding and seemingly endless grievances of the black community lest dire, yet "understandable," consequences ensue -- as though opposition to welfare programs that have failed in the past were an act of racial prejudice worthy of punishment.

No one can doubt the truth of the proposition that race is a burden on the American conscience. No one would deny that the legal and institutional discrimination that was the legacy of American Slavery, required a national rethinking and a dramatic redress. But it has been a quarter of a century since the agonizing reappraisal and restitution took place. Why is America's conscience about race still the subject of such passionate attacks? Why are Americans -- surely the most diverse, tolerant, and generous of people -- constantly being accused by their media and leaders of boundless racist sentiments and acts of oppression?

After all, most Americans over 30 have participated in, or supported, a political and cultural revolution without parallel in human history. In a single generation, discriminatory practices and segregationist laws in America have been declared unconstitutional and universally abolished. Martin Luther King, the black leader of this struggle to create civil equality for all Americans, is now a national hero -- along with Washington and Lincoln, the only American to be specially honored with a national holiday. His dream of a future in which every individual would be "judged by the content of his character and not the color of his skin" has been integrated into the American dream in a way that only Lincoln's famous Gettysburg image -- "a government of, by, and for the people" -- had been previously.

As dramatic as America's homage to Dr. King has been, its commitment to provide black Americans with full citizenship rights has been no less striking. Black Americans have become the mayors, police chiefs, and public officials of Birmingham, Selma, Atlanta, the very citadels of what was once the segregationist South. The mayor of Atlanta is himself a former civil rights activist, a lieutenant of Dr. King and a onetime U.S. Ambassador to the United Nations.

At the root of this paradox is a new politically inspired racism. While the old racism may have served economic and social interests, its root sources were instinctive and visceral. White crackers, Ku Klux Klanners, and assorted neo-Nazis of the old school believed in the genetic inferiority of other groups and yearned to be rid of them -- or failing that -- to repress them. This is the racism that America fought wars against abroad and defeated at home.

But there is a new racism rampant in America today. It is politically inspired and seeks the enactment of laws that are racially specific and tailored to the requirements of selected groups; it attributes the economic, social, and moral problems of designated minorities to their alleged "oppression" by a rigged system; and it seeks to solve their problems by the exaction of public ransoms in the form of government benefits and special privilege for ethnic grievance. This new racism has sprung up and spread like a poisonous weed to choke the civility that the civil rights movement established. It has given the old racism a new lease on life.

The function of a civil order is to humanize the behavior of its citizens and elevate their souls, to restrain their impulses to savagery and evil. That is the significance of the laws that were instituted by the civil rights revolution under the leadership of Martin Luther King. By making America's standards color blind and universal, they completed the constitutional covenant and reaffirmed its principles and ideals: they called America to its better self.

But it was never in their capacity to remake Americans, to extirpate the reflexes of fear and resentment of the other that achieve their repulsive apotheosis in racism, and that are inscribed in the character of all human beings like a malignant genetic code. Just as the impulse to sin does not disappear with religion, so barbarism does not vanish with civilization: It can only be held at bay and driven underground. The old racism did not die with the advent of the civil rights revolution, and this is why defending its principles is more urgent than ever.

For these principles are now under siege by the new political racism, whose malignancy rises from the Marxist cauldrons of the radical Left. Its immediate target is white "establishment" America, but its ultimate victims are poor and black.

America became familiar with the voice of this racism in a series of controversial criminal investigations in which racial issues were pushed to the fore. In the most memorable of these -- the Howard Beach and Tawana Brawley incidents -- the pattern was identical: A racial crime was committed -- or, in the case of Tawana Brawley who claimed to have been raped and mutilated by a gang of whites, allegedly committed. But in each case the law was blocked in its efforts to investigate the circumstances of the crimes. And in each case, the forces that blocked their efforts were the radical attorneys for the victims themselves. They refused to allow their clients to cooperate with the law in the prosecution of the crimes, claiming justice would not be done, indeed could not be done, because the system was in its very nature racist and unjust. Thus, the crimes became the occasions not for indictments of the deranged individuals who might have actually committed them, but of America itself. (Did these accusations seem like the paranoid responses of the political fringe? Tawana Brawley and her lawyers, later exposed by investigators as liars and frauds, were supported by a broad based public in the black community including celebrities like Bill Cosby, who donated tens of thousands of dollars to their cause.)

The indictment of America as a racist oppressor has been heard before. It is the prosecutorial brief of the radical Left. In the 1960s it was the legal strategy of every radical on trial from Panther leader and murderer Huey Newton to the guerilla conspirators of the "Chicago 7." Newton's Marxist lawyer, Charles Garry, who devised the defense strategy of "putting the system on trial" titled his autobiography *Streetfighter in the Courtroom*. When Bobby Seale and a group of Black Panthers in New Haven, Connecticut, were indicted for the torture-murder of Alex Rackley, student radicals at Yale shut down the University and demanded that their trial be stopped. So fevered was the political atmosphere of the time, that these student nihilists were actually supported by Yale President Kingman Brewster, who explained to the media that "a black person cannot get a fair trial in America today." (This turned out to be a true statement if the black person, like Alex Rackley, had the misfortune of being murdered by the Left. Though they had admitted participating in the torture, the Panther leaders were not convicted.)

The radical lawyers for Tawana Brawley and the Howard Beach defendants -- Vernon Mason and Alton Maddox -- learned their courtroom strategies during the Sixties in the liberation schools of the radical Left. Both Mason and Maddox were trained by William Kuntsler, undisputed dean of "revolutionary" lawyers -- comrade-in-arms and advocate for Abbie

Hoffman, Tom Hayden, and the "Chicago 7" (whom he collectively compared to Jesus Christ), attorney and political sympathizer for the cop-killing terrorists of the Black Liberation Army, and today counsellor for the "wilding" rapists of Central Park.

It is because the new racism is a bastard child of the political Left that it has gone largely unnoted by social commentators and generally unreported in the nation's press. There are historical grounds for this myopia. Racist movements have long been associated in the public mind with the political Right, while the Left has been seen as a champion of oppressed minorities and civil rights. But even these facile associations reflect a distorted perspective. Thus "populism," the most successful leftist movement in America's past, eventually degenerated into segregationist politics, while Nazism, the most significant racist movement of the 20th Century (though generally labelled a movement of the Right), was radically anti-capitalist and socialist from the start.

A more solid ground for the impression that the Right is properly associated with racial politics while the Left pursues goals of social integration is the history of the civil rights revolution itself. Although the old Marxist Left had once advocated black separatism and a "black nation" (to be made up of several states in the American South), it changed its attitude for opportunistic reasons in the 1940s and '50s and provided crucial support for the integrationist push. It is also true that most conservatives, defending the principles of states' rights and private contract, initially opposed the civil rights revolution and thus lent their political weight to the old racism in its last ditch stand.

But the last 25 years have brought dramatic changes in the political landscape affecting both Right and Left, at home and abroad. The civil rights revolution is now a long accomplished fact, ratified in America's social consciousness and solidly inscribed in American law. American conservatives not only have come to accept the wisdom of the revolution they once resisted, but have become its staunchest political defenders. In battle after battle over affirmative action proposals and other post-civil rights efforts by liberals to introduce racial categories and quotas into laws of the land, it is conservative legislators who have insisted that the law be "color blind" and it is conservative presidents and Supreme Court justices who have attempted through their veto power to hold the line.

But more important even than these changes in the complexion of the political Right have been the changes that have taken place on the political Left. No sooner was the civil rights revolution written into law than the radical Left was agitating to overthrow it. Integration was derided as "Uncle Tomism" and "co-optation;" "black power" became the slogan of the radical agenda. Martin Luther King was now a legend of the discarded past; Malcolm X was the prophet of the radical future.

This progression was inevitable. Radicals are the permanently unsatisfied among us, the resentful nihilists of the utopian cause. Restless with the imperfections of humanity as they find it, radicals clamor for a future in which human beings will be different and the world will be transformed. In the radical future, racism and other evils will be miraculously purged from the species forever, and of course the radicals themselves will inherit the earth. But first society must be polarized and all existing structures destroyed. This is the secular messianism that has blighted our century, the malevolent "idealism" that subverts its own ends and leads instead to the Nazi gas chambers and the Communist gulag.

For old style liberals and contemporary conservatives, politics is fundamentally the art of compromise. For radicals it is war by other means. The civil war of radical politics begins by dividing society into opposing camps: victims and victimizers, oppressors and oppressed. This war can end only with the annihilation of the social enemy, which ushers in the millenium of social peace.

In launching a civil war in which victory must be total, radicalism reveals itself as a species of racism. Communism and fascism are kissing cousins: the stigmatization of entire social groups, whether capitalists or Jews, is combined with the will to suppress them permanently in the name of a better world.

Marxism long appeared to be free from racist taint because the messianic force on which it pinned its hopes was not an ethnic or racial group, but an economic class. But in the 1960s, radicals lost all hope that the working class would ever become a revolutionary force. Instead, they transferred their destructive faith to substitute candidates: women, gays, and blacks. It was in this crucible that radical feminism, and the gay and black liberation movements of the New Left were forged.

In the American South, the emergence of this Left, under the leadership of Stokely Carmichael and the black power activists, derailed the integration process and the civil rights agenda. Guided by radicals like Carmichael, the Movement that had once fought for an integrated America became anti-white and anti-Semitic and anti-American as well.

Martin Luther King had believed in American democracy, and had fought for a single American standard: one justice indivisible, for all. He had embraced the historic alliance between blacks and Jews, America's other outcast minority and championed the cause of American pluralism. Carmichael hated America and American democracy, hated Jews and hated whites and expelled them from the civil rights coalition, preaching black separatism and black power. The goal of integration -- the classic route to success in America -- was condemned by the new black radicals as a path to moral corruption and political co-option; the path of equal opportunity was dismissed as a mirage; the strategies of non-violence and compromise were rejected in favor of a politics of confrontation and threat; the political model of the civil rights struggle ceased to be one of moral suasion and became one of civil war.

At the end of the '60s when violent revolution failed to materialize, Carmichael deserted his constituents and went into exile as a prince across the water in Marxist Guinea. In his adopted homeland, the atrocities committed by the government against its impoverished African population were acceptable to him because the dictator was a friend, a socialist and black. But in the last decade, as the seeds he had sown in the '60s began to sprout their poisonous blooms, Carmichael returned to spread his message of anti-Americanism, anti-Semitism, and black racism on campuses across the United States, where he was welcomed by the New Left professoriate and its student disciples.

For two decades, activists like Carmichael have been stars of the campus circuit, indoctrinating new generations in the divisive and racially polarizing ideologies of the radical Left, and in denigrating American values and institutions. They have been supported by a chorus of white New Left academics and accommodating administrators who find their rantings congenial. Indeed, the universities themselves have been transformed by the New Left into staging areas for the radical future.

When the guerrillas of the '60s marched off the streets and into the universities at the end of the decade, they did not demand "proletarian studies" programs to advance their Marxist class agendas. Instead they demanded Black Studies, Women's Studies, Native American Studies, and

Gay and Lesbian Studies. These new "disciplines," for which there were no intellectual standards or academic traditions, provided an ideal proving ground for their revised ideologies of political warfare -- feminism, black nationalism, and gay liberation. Rather than becoming institutions of scholarly research, the new "Studies Centers" became intellectual fortresses from which to launch new assaults on America's values and American culture.

In the 1960s Amiri Baraka, a.k.a. Leroi Jones, was a radical loud-mouth, writing diatribes like this: "We want poems like fists beating niggers out of Jocks of dagger poems in the slimy bellies of the owner-jews/Look at the Liberal Spokesman for the jews clutch his throat and puke himself into eternity/Another bad poem cracking steel knuckles in a jewlady's mouth." Today, thanks to the new cultural diversity in the American Academy, Amiri Baraka is chairman of the Afro-American Studies Department at the prestigious Stonybrook campus of the State University of New York. At Stonybrook, Baraka has found a tenured platform from which to denounce America and to praise its global enemies. Nor is he untypical. Cornel West is a professor of "Afro-American Studies" at Princeton University, earning perhaps $70,000 a year. Writing in the Leftist magazine *Tikkun* recently, Professor West described himself as "an Afro-American freedom fighter." While this is revealing of the rich fantasy life of the professorial left, it also reflects its sinister agenda: to convince black students that America is a racist oppressor and that the real solution is war.

It is this campus Left that has promulgated the idea that there is no common cultural heritage that belongs to all Americans; that the culture out of which this democracy was conceived is really the culture of a master race; that the American consensus is oppressive in its very nature, in the same way that American justice is oppressive, that American institutions are inherently racist and need to be replaced.

The appeal to philosophical principle and abstract theory is the high road taken by New Left academics in their assault on the covenants that, until now, have made America's democracy the wonder and envy of the world. But there is a low road, as well, on which popular demagogues have followed after them, inspired by their indictments and encouraged by their attacks. From Susan Sontag's infamous thesis of the 1960s that "The white race is the cancer of history" to Black Muslim Elijah Muhammad's revelation that whites are devils invented by a mad scientist named Yakub, is no great leap at all.

The largest and most powerful racist organization in the United States today is the Nation of Islam, a pseudo-religious political cult, founded by Louis Farrakhan and born out of the same malevolent crucible as the '60s Left. Today, Farrakhan is a favorite campus speaker of Black Student Unions across the country, commanding $10,000 fees for spreading his gospel of racist pride and hate. For Farrakhan, as for the liberation theologians of the radical Left, the political is religious. Thus, he and his followers regard white America and its Jews as great Satans conspiring to commit genocide against the black population through the epidemics of drugs and AIDS. In a recent speech broadcast as a public service by the leftist Pacifica station KPFK, Farrakhan lieutenant Steve Coakely even identified the local measles epidemic in Los Angeles as part of this genocidal plot.

In his diatribe, Coakely also touched a radical theme that has been showcased for national audiences in Spike Lee's *Do the Right Thing*. Coakley claimed that white America was killing blacks with impunity. The problem with black people, he complained, was that "we don't deliver retribution," which could also be a subtext of Lee's film. ("Tawana Brawley Told The Truth" was a slogan scrawled across one of its frames.)

At a recent public gathering in the heart of the nation's capital, with former civil rights hero and disgraced Mayor Marion Barry on the podium as an object lesson, "Minister Farrakhan" worked his black audience preparing them for the coming race war. Invoking the "persecution" of American blacks over the centuries, he pointed to Barry as the most recent example and ranted: "All white America could be asked to die to equal the score."

Racist hatemongers like Farrakhan and Coakely, and their genocidal messages, far from being stigmatized and isolated on the political fringe, have -- through the intervention of the political Left, the tolerance of the civil rights establishment, and the acquiescence of the liberal center -- become part of the culture itself. The claim that there is a governmental/white conspiracy against blacks in America has been a weapon in the rhetorical arsenal of the Left for two decades. It is as readily found in the editorials of the leftist *Nation* (which have routinely claimed that the war on drugs is a war on black America), as in the public utterances of literary icons like Toni Morrison, who told *Time* magazine that the only thing binding America together, as a nation, was its racism towards American blacks.

Embracing the general idea of genocidal conspiracy supported by radical academic theorists, obviously makes it easier to accept the specific paranoias spread by demagogues like Farrakhan about drugs and AIDS. But the grotesque libels have themselves been propounded by tenured radicals as though they were facts, and disseminated in "news" stories by leftwing journalists like Earl Caldwell of New York's *Daily News*. Even as responsible a black columnist as William Raspberry of *The Washington Post* has defended Farrakhan on the spurious grounds that he has some true things to say (as though Hitler did not). Nor has the outcry against these genocidal libels been all that deafening. Jesse Jackson, while still the leading Democratic politician in Chicago, chose to be silent during the public storm that broke after it was revealed that Coakely -- then a $70,000 a year aide to the Democratic Mayor -- had accused Jewish doctors of injecting blacks with AIDS. Widely regarded as a moral leader, Jackson can condemn the President of the United States as a racist, while refusing to make similar judgements about Coakely, the Nation of Islam or Farrakhan, his continuing friend and political ally.

Silences like Jackson's are made easy and thus virtually inevitable by the liberal center's collusive tolerance of the new racism. This tolerance ranges from allowing political demagogues to posture as moral spokesmen while maintaining their ties to bigots like Farrakhan, to portraying those bigots as social critics. Thus a *New York Times* story described Washington Mayor Marion Barry's alliance with Farrakhan in these self-parodying terms: "[Barry] has shown up at rallies with the Rev. Louis Farrakhan, the Nation of Islam leader who has gained nationwide attention for his criticism of white society, particularly Jews."

Mayor Barry's alliance with Farrakhan was but the latest episode in the series of Reichstag fire incidents that began with the fraudulent claims of Tawana Brawley and escalated afterwards, in which the normal processes of the judicial system are converted by leftwing racists and black "nationalists" into their standard morality play about oppressive "Amerikkka" ruled by white devils and in need of liberation. The success of this morality play is such that the truly genocidal libel that whites and Jews are plotting the destruction of black Americans is now given wide credence in black communities across the country, in the way similar conspiracy libels against the CIA and other government agencies have become staples of belief in the communities of the Left.

A recent *Los Angeles Times* report on the spread of conspiracy theories in the black community quoted Wilbert Tatum, editor and publisher of New York's oldest and largest black paper, the *Amsterdam News*, as believing that the federal government was involved in a secret plot with Latin American drug kingpins and Mafia bosses to flood inner-city neighborhoods with narcotics as a form of genocide against blacks. When asked for evidence, Tatum could only cite the "authentic language" of a scene in "The Godfather" in which a Mafia don decides to push drugs to blacks. William Cavil, associate director of the Institute for Advanced Study of Black Family Life and Culture in Oakland, California, was quoted in the same report as saying "I don't understand, if there's not some conspiracy going on, how every group has managed to flourish and get ahead in the country except African-Americans," and Barbara Sizemore, a black studies professor at the University of Pittsburgh, as concluding "I no longer think it's a conspiracy ... I call it outright war."

The conquest of the political culture of the black community by the political culture of the radical Left has allowed hatemongers like Farrakhan to gain an acceptance and support among blacks that is truly alarming. It far exceeds the acceptance of any comparable figure including the most popular social prophet among today's black youth, the late Malcolm X. Although it is generally forgotten now, during his lifetime Malcolm X was condemned and isolated by Martin Luther King and the broad leadership of the black civil rights movement precisely because of his rhetorical violence and racist agendas. (And with positive effect: In the last years of his life, Malcolm abandoned the racist creed of his Black Muslim past.)

The liberal center is now so permeated by the culture of the Left that institutions like the *Times* and *The Washington Post* (which recently presented Farrakhan's views in a lengthy, respectful format suited to a world important statesman) are unable to recognize the enemies of liberal society for what they are. As a result, they legitimize by default "community leaders" whose civic agenda is to provoke a race war. Of course, this liberal myopia applies only to hatemongers in one direction. Grand Dragons of the Ku Klux Klan and Neo-Nazis, with parallel ideas, can expect no such respectful receptions.

The double standard has led to other ugly consequences: the legitimization of white racist rhetoric in the advocacy of reverse affirmative action among ordinary Americans who don't necessarily read the *Times*; the re-emergence of white racism as a political program in the candidacy of former klansman David Duke. In a political atmosphere in which preferential treatment and race-based laws are advocated by the liberal establishment, a National Association for the Advancement of White People can begin to look like an equal opportunity party.

In fact, this revitalization of the old racism is integral to the agenda of the Left, because it is the key to its favored strategy, which is to eliminate the moderate center. Thus, in the early '70s, Angela Davis formed a Communist Party front called the Alliance Against Racism whose main target was the Ku Klux Klan. At the time, the Klan was a thoroughly discredited, closely monitored, and generally moribund institution. Shortly afterwards, a mini-sect calling itself the Communist Workers Party announced a "Death to the Klan" rally in Greensboro, North Carolina, provoking a gun battle in which five of their own members were killed. At the time, the Klan was hardly important. But it was vital to the political strategy of leftists like Angela Davis and the Communist Workers Party that the Klan be important. For it is only when the political situation becomes polarized that the radical agenda can begin to seem reasonable to ordinary people.

Historically, in fact, the way to every leftist political victory has been paved by the elimination of the political middle. Only when the Left can present itself as the lone alternative to a facist Right has victory been within its grasp. In the last two decades, the Left has greatly eroded the liberal center on the issue of race. The Democratic Party has been almost completely captured by the agenda of affirmative action and racial preference. In California, the Democratic candidate for governor in 1990 began her campaign by declaring that she would staff her administration according to racial quotas. For nearly three decades, the Left has relentlessly assaulted the American ethos -- the idea of universal standards, of equal opportunity, and of competitive reward. The task that faces Americans is to defend those principles by reaffirming their faith in American justice, by condemning and isolating racist hatemongers, and by rejecting the radical Left, both black and white, which uses politics as a means of civil war.

15

The Promise of America

William Allen

By now the question, "What ever happened to civil rights in the United States?" is pervasive. The question seems to assume a problem at least in perception -- namely, that the civil rights movement that climaxed in the 1960s has run aground. Inasmuch as the objectives of the original civil rights movement were not fully realized, this observation is cause for alarm. Inasmuch as the objectives were fully realized, but advocates for civil rights remain organized and continue to press their concerns upon the nation's agenda, this is a source of perplexity. Thus, the curious and the anxious unite in seeking to explain the altered social and political climate.

Among the several attempts to respond to this query, none is perhaps more ill-advised than the one that tries to locate civil rights somewhere mid-stream in an evolving constitutional tradition. In that view, the objectives of the civil rights movement can no more be fully realized in any given epoch than can a biological species, in any given epoch, become fully evolved. The notion makes no sense, for the objectives, the ends, evolve no less surely than do the means to their realization.

A noted exponent of this view is Harvard Law Professor Derrick Bell. In a 1988 symposium on the "Afro-American and the Evolution of the Living Constitution" Professor Bell defended the view, arguing that the original constitutional tradition was innocent of any concern for civil rights, per se. He quoted Governor Morris declaiming at the Constitutional Convention that "the protection of property is the end of government." Morris of course recanted that statement just as soon as the question of slavery arose. He recanted because he did not want to extend that consideration to slavery. Professor Bell, however, gave credit to Morris neither in his symposium remarks nor in his book, *And We Are Not Saved*, from which he drew the remarks.[1]

Why Bell thought it appropriate to create a misleading impression of this Founding Father I do not know. For many others, however, the same result derives from a pernicious view of the country as locked in class warfare. The exponents of this view end up borrowing, whether knowingly or not, from the concordance of Karl Marx. When Bell quoted Morris as saying that "the aim of this society is the protection of property," he produced the impression of a conscious, bourgeois plot to exploit a proletariat. Morris, however, did not declare the protection of property to be the aim of *this* society, he rather asserted the general principle that the protection of property is the aim of civil society. From this general principle he meant to deduce the relevant specific applications for the United States. Before he had gotten very far in that process he had to recant, as we have seen. He had discovered that the existence of chattel slavery within the United States complicated the analysis, and he refused to permit his general theory of human nature to lend aid and comfort to the claims of property in human beings.

To employ class analysis as a stand-in for race in attempting to understand American politics is doubly misguided. First, it hinges on a weak argument -- the defense of class analysis -- and, second, it serves to obscure the unique and significant role that race has played in United States history. I have discussed the latter question at length in a recently published essay.[2] The former -- the weakness of class analysis itself -- deserves a few pages in this context precisely because of its familiar connection with the question of race.

Americans came to the language of "class analysis," "pluralism," and "multiculturalism" in a context far broader than the relation of American blacks to the constitutional tradition. Earlier in this century Charles Beard argued that the Federalists, and most notably people like Alexander Hamilton, were defenders of a propertied class. Beard, of course, was more subtle than that. He examined the Constitutional Convention's delegate list and divided the delegates according to the kinds of property the individuals held.

---

[1] New York, Basic Books, 1987. pp. 29-33.

[2] "A New Birth of Freedom: Fulfillment or Derailment," in **Slavery and Its Consequences: The Constitution, Equality, and Race**, ed. by Robert A. Goldwin and Art Kaufman (Washington, D. C.: American Enterprise Institute, 1988).

The chief division Beard employed was between "realty" and "personalty." Wealth held in the form of realty is most fundamentally landed wealth, or wealth not readily movable. Personalty is primarily money, securities; that is, wealth that is easily movable and, indeed, which becomes wealth in a certain sense only by being transferred. Beard concluded that the Federalists (who were the nationalists) were mainly folk who held personalty, which is not to say that they possessed no other assets but that their wealth was not concentrated in large landholdings (except for western lands, subject to considerable speculation, and which had more to do with noteholding than with land ownership). The Federalists also dominated the Constitutional Convention, and, presumably, they operated in the interests of people like themselves, with commercial interests.

The Beardian thesis was developed particularly in relation to *The Federalist Papers*. In his analysis, the tenth *Federalist* defended a system designed to restrain the majority, so that people who held movable wealth could protect themselves from the other classes in society. When Beard's book appeared,[3] there had not been for several years any extensive scholarship on *The Federalist Papers*. Beard re-ignited a fascination with those essays and especially with the tenth essay.

Many people followed in his path. As one would expect, however, it was not long before the other side had its hearing, and the counter-Beardian thesis began to emerge. The central question was already stated in *The Federalist* Number One; namely, whether people's motivations in politics and society can be assumed from the identity of their material or class interests. Can one attribute to someone a specific end or purpose simply because of his identified material status? From the knowledge that someone holds substantial securities, can one make the leap to the conclusion that his political opinions support the activities of the stock market or of people who, like himself, hold such securities?

In the scholarly literature, the argument has by now shifted away from the Beardian model and its assumptions. It has done so for two reasons: first, Beard miscalculated the property-holdings and votes of delegates to the Constitutional Convention. In fact, persons of all kinds of property were on all sides of the debate over the Constitution (and the debate over slavery). Second, it became clear that the Beardian model did not eliminate the need

---

[3] An Economic Interpretation of the Constitution (1913).

to understand and articulate the positions people actually took (witness the discussion of Governor Morris above). Thus, there seemed not to be much promise in the Beardian model. Despite that, many persons still stubbornly cling to it. We need to ask both why it pleased people initially and why, in some cases, it still does so.

The Beardian model was essentially an attempt to apply to the American experience an analytic model that had prevailed primarily in the discussion of European politics -- a politics which does focus fundamentally on class and status to this very day. This mode of analysis was given its decisive form in the works of Karl Marx in the nineteenth century, beginning with his youthful *Economic and Philosophical Manuscripts* and continuing through such mature works as *The Communist Manifesto*. Marxist class-based analysis presupposed a distinction between the proletariat and the bourgeoisie, and a necessary historical confrontation between the two. Insofar as this coming historical confrontation was a scientific fact -- as Marx presented it -- it had to apply to all human beings everywhere. The inspiration for the Beardian analysis was the belief that this "scientific fact" did indeed pertain to America. Patient reflection and research would uncover it. Arthur Bentley was a contemporary of Beard. Bentley gave us the term "pluralism" as a social descriptor. There is perhaps no more frequently used descriptor of American social and political life today.

Bentley was engaged in the same project that engrossed Beard, though from a slightly different angle. Bentley maintained that to ground the analysis and description of American political life in terms that explain human political associations universally, it is necessary to find terms of description that apply everywhere and not just in America. The term, "pluralistic," was his way of dealing with the way in which the class struggle was "disguised" in America behind groups or factions which were the fundamental facts of representation in the United States.

What is meant by "fundamental facts of representation" is that Americans participate in politics and social life primarily, if not exclusively, through affinity groupings. (They do not participate as individuals, according to the theory.) This concurs with the Marxian assumption that the individual has no standing in the social realm. The individual is either the capitalist or the proletarian (the laborer) for Marx, and assumes a different name (such as black) to express the same phenomenon for pluralism. The laborer's interests are expressed not by the laborer as an individual but by the group -- labor.

These are the underlying principles of Bentley's notion of pluralism, which analyzes the political system on the basis of the relative position of affinity groups in society. These principles, in turn, became the foundation for elitist theory which starts from the proposition that while affinity groups may take precedence in society, someone has to speak for them. But no matter how sophisticated the refinements become, the groups in Bentley's pluralism are only modified and disguised versions of Marx's classes. As a consequence of these we are led to a fairly general expectation that all politics is based on adherence to some class interest. Based on such recent notions, scholars frequently return to the era of the Founding Fathers to judge its accomplishments in terms of the affinity groups of the Founders themselves.

The first and most important harmful consequence of this attitude toward the past is its power to blind us to the reality which actually unfolded. When we attempt to make the past conform to our present understanding, we deny ourselves the opportunity to learn from it. When we dismiss Governor Morris as a mere advocate of eighteenth century capitalism, we deny ourselves all access to those views which persuaded Governor Morris of the evil of slavery. That would perhaps appear to us less a harmful consequence, if we possessed as alternative a certain guide or principle by which we could readily persuade one another of slavery's evil. But our contemporary culture offers no such guide or principle.

Without the arguments from the Founding era, we are at a loss to establish any moral authority for the condemnation of slavery. Without these underlying principles the Thirteenth Amendment to the Constitution would have no more meaning for us than a majority vote, registered at a certain historical moment, and capable of being rescinded at any time another majority may so wish. I maintain, therefore, that our attitude in interpreting the past ought to be a willingness to approach the Constitution and its architects as if these were individuals standing before us whose arguments and interests we will take at face value -- initially if not completely. Then we can investigate them and determine what it is they sought to accomplish and what import that has for us.

It may not appear at first that such academic concerns have much to do with the subject of this volume. However, it is reasoning such as this that is responsible for the wrong turn we took some years back, when we combined the politics of civil rights with the politics of poverty -- when we confused the issue of justice for all with the issue of relief for the poor. That move predisposed us to develop a policy that would treat minorities -- blacks in particular -- as specific objects of governmental concern and manipulation.

When "simple justice" called not for treating *all* commonly, but rather for commonly distinguishing *some*, then did we step on the slippery slope. We officially divided the country into Americans and aliens, the aliens being persons who were the specific objects of Americans' caring. For a time we even forgot that there were poor people besides blacks, so much had the terms black and poor become synonymous. By the time we had been reminded by other groups -- women, Asians, Hispanics, the handicapped, etc. -- clambering for Great Society largess, it was too late. Our policies meant targeted relief for the needy, *not* justified recognition of the worthy! The psychology of charity had come to dominate what ought to have been a psychology of humanity, a psychology of responsible citizenship, with the result that whoever came to be touched by it came thereby to be stigmatized as deficient.

The foregoing discussion elucidates the kind of ambiguities that fundamental criticism would give us the opportunity to work through. If we are serious about our work, we should never undertake such a discussion without planning to challenge ourselves to the utmost. To conduct that kind of challenge, we should be willing to put something at risk. It would require that we imagine the possibility that we could benefit occasionally from being shown to be incorrect. I believe there are reasons today to take that attitude to heart, more perhaps than ever before, because I think there is real ground to ponder whether the fundamental movement of civil rights in America has not run aground.

It is fair to say that the people of the United States today are more race conscious than at any other time in the history of the United States. That statement will be more shocking to some than to others, but it ought to be a disappointment to everyone. It ought especially to disappoint us when we reflect that we witness race consciousness today in places where we least expect it. On the American campus of higher education, of all places, and then in those very institutions which only 20 years ago were the very emblems of progressive, indeed, radical thought, we watch the dream of racial harmony gradually disintegrate before our very eyes.

When I insist, therefore, that the civil rights movement may have run aground, I do not seek to be confused with individuals who maintain that "the civil rights movement is over, accomplished; the questions have been resolved." Instead, I think it has run aground, not merely short of its goal but set in the wrong direction. We are insufficiently aware of the resources that can aid us and insufficiently aware of the contributions that we must make in order to survive. For example, we have been willing to leave as a mere matter of taste, of commitment, the conclusion that discrimination and slavery are unjust. To do that is to refuse to defend our principles, and therefore to fail to give them any chance of success. To pass these principles off as "value judgments," mere arbitrary assertions, means we ourselves do not conceive of them as defensible in the court of reason and of political deliberation. Failing to present that defense, we fail not only ourselves but also humanity.

It is too late for the Smithsonian symposium to approach this work seriously, but not too late for others. One thing is clear: the vision of a society of distinct, competing, and heterogeneous groups will always be inadequate to the articulation of a concept of citizenship that views the whole society as one. We need at least that much: a new articulation of citizenship, not a recapitulation of the old statements.

Among the things we would be able to see once we achieved this articulation would be the extent to which general confusion colors our discussions of the Constitution and especially civil rights laws. We "enjoy" nearly 150 federal statutes regarding civil rights, not always mutually compatible and sometimes outright contradictory among themselves. Though Congress assigns title and chapter numbers to these acts, the fact is that the entire edifice has not been reviewed with a comprehensive eye since 1875! No one -- no one in the entire country -- can say with any confidence that he knows what his civil rights are. We owe the people a clear understanding of what their rights are at a minimum, even if we cannot guarantee their full enjoyment. We will not be aided in fulfilling this objective by language that envisions an open-ended, fluid process which is always being newly defined, evolving, and never bound to deliver any of its past promises.

We can most clearly understand the danger inherent in an evolutionary view of our Constitution and laws by looking at another aspect of the century-long battle to establish a colorblind Constitution. In that struggle, the goal has always been such blessings of liberty as were enjoyed by

Englishmen and Americans from time immemorial. In the era of Reconstruction the Congress even spoke, in its statutes, of the "same rights as white men enjoy." The problem, however, is how to define those rights. If we assume them to be constantly evolving, then we can have no fixed standard to aim at. The rights which white men enjoyed yesterday may not be the rights white men enjoy tomorrow. That not insignificant ambiguity has enabled the defenders of an evolutionary Constitution to tease American blacks, and others, with the lure of an equality which remains permanently undefined. We have never been in a position to point to any particular arrangement as fulfilling the promise, but the authority of every prior arrangement is denied by the idea of evolution. Lincoln was able to refer back four score and seven years to a "standard maxim" of a free society precisely because he did not hold to an evolutionary view. The equality of the Declaration of Independence was to him a fixed compass point. Accordingly, it was possible to state what adjustments would repair the injuries of the past. When the compass point is removed, the ability to measure progress is no less removed.

We see this most clearly in the area of the claims of American blacks claims for redress for the injuries of slavery and discrimination. Under the traditional practices of Anglo-American jurisprudence, it was a simple matter to envision a tortious jurisprudence that could handle the problem. Under a non-traditional, evolutionary standard, however, the courthouse doors have been closed to significant tortious settlements or judgments. Instead, elaborate administrative and bureaucratic procedures have been installed -- the latest advances in the technology of assigning blacks their proper places in society. The evidence is still coming in, as scholarship reviews the past hundred years in this respect. But already it is not too early to announce the conclusion.

In spite of the explosion of civil rights laws, the loud protestations of concern, and the elaborate social and political structures established to implement these concerns, American blacks have been systematically excluded from the traditional guarantees of Anglo-American jurisprudence and constitutionalism. In the space of merely a decade, for example, we have seen the area of law called "sexual harassment" carved out and enabled to become an effective tool for litigating civil rights complaints -- with significant judgments and settlements -- while the older, more solidly established category, "racial harassment," remains vaguely articulated and of ambiguous legal status. It is difficult to resist the conclusion that the difference between the two is closely tied to the problem of race.

In other areas the results are analogous. Two years ago, in fact, a family of three youths afflicted with the HIV infection won a $1.1 million settlement from a school district on their complaint of unfair treatment resulting from the exclusion of the youths from the school. The complaint was a civil rights complaint, and the family had just cause to complain. It is nevertheless the case that their complaint was almost exactly analogous with the complaints of millions of American blacks for more than one hundred years. And nowhere in that long history will the records disclose even a single black citizen, on no less just complaints, receiving any judgment or settlement even remotely similar. Indeed, poor Linda Brown, whose 1954 case purportedly created a revolution in our law, not only won no damages but never even got to attend the school involved!

The point of these reflections is not to generate a host of new tort filings. It is rather to demonstrate that we have systematically attempted to vindicate civil rights for a generation now without recourse to the most powerful tool Anglo-American jurisprudence knows, a far more powerful deterrent than affirmative action and its system of paper compliance. In other words, the system we have "evolved" in this respect has above all else worked to deny the just claims of citizenship of countless American blacks. A traditional view of our Constitution and laws would not have made that mistake. The civil rights movement ran aground because of its rejection of a traditional view of our Constitution. The unfinished agenda is primarily to reestablish the claims of American blacks to be legitimate heirs to the Founding Fathers.

In this regard I would ask you to ponder three images which for me have long expressed the character of the choices we face. The first image derives from the *Old Testament*, in which Naboth is summoned by King Ahab and requested to sell his vineyard; as you know, Naboth said, "No, no, no, God forbid." Naboth's relationship to his forefathers was such that he could not conceive of surrendering that patrimony -- "God forbid." A second tale of vineyards derives from the *New Testament*. It is the tale of the ungrateful tenants who received a property from the master, only then to refuse him the rent they owed. The master sent the rent collector, but they slew him. Next he sent his son, but they slew him also. The master then said, "What am I to do? I must go myself," and the ungrateful tenants exclaimed, "God forbid."

The third tale derives not from the holy text but from Aesop'*s Fables.* It is the tale of the father who, on his deathbed, summoned his sons about him and said, "I am going to die now, but I want you to know that there is a treasure buried in the vineyard." The boys saw the father to his death with full respect, but as soon as that was done they betook themselves to the vineyard with shovel and spade. They did not find trunks filled with jewels or gems. Disheartened, they imagined that their father had deceived them, promising so much and delivering so little. That fall, however, they discovered to their delight that they enjoyed the most wonderful harvest they had ever seen.

I often think, when I hear people speak about the principles of the Constitution, that they are trying to decide whether they must choose and, if so, which of these three postures they should strike in regard to that legacy. I, for one, have no trouble setting my course.

When we speak of the "evolution" of the Constitution and the status of American blacks in the United States, we must never imagine that, like Topsy, it just happened. There is nothing inevitable in the development of the United States, nor in the realization of the promise of freedom for black men. This rare and difficult achievement of a free society of many races was won and is still being won only at the cost of innumerable cares, labors, and dangers. Americans are in fact building, and always have been, a polity worthy of its original Constitution, of the intention of the Founding Fathers -- a polity respectful of the dignity of all human beings, not in the abstract but in the concrete expression of an abiding confidence that there are nowhere men who are not capable of self-government.

Selected Bibliography

Affirmative Discrimination by Nathan Glaser (Harvard University Press; Cambridge, Massachusetts; 1987)

Broken Alliance: The Turbulent Times Between Blacks and Jews in America by Jonathan Kaufman (Scribner's, Charles, Sons; New York, New York; 1988)

Civil Rights: Rhetoric or Reality by Thomas Sowell (Morrow, William, & Co., Inc.; New York, New York; 1985)

The Closest of Strangers by Jim Sleeper (Norton, W.W., & Co., Inc.; New York, New York; 1990)

The Content of Our Character by Shelby Steele (St. Martin's Press; New York, New York; 1990)

The Declining Significance of Race by William J. Wilson (University of Chicago Press; Chicago, Illinois; 1980)

Ethnic America: A History by Thomas Sowell (Basic Bks., Inc.; New York, New York; 1981)

Eyes on the Prize: America's Civil Rights Years, 1954-1965 by Juan Williams (Viking Press; New York, New York; 1987)

The Limits of Social Policy by Nathan Glaser (Harvard University Press; Cambridge, Massachusetts; 1988)

Losing Ground by Charles Murray (Basic Bks., Inc., New York, New York; 1984)

Lovesong by Julius Lester (Henry Holt & Co.; New York, New York; 1988)

Notes of a Hanging Judge by Stanley Crouch (Oxford University Press; New York, New York; 1990)

Preferential Policies by Thomas Sowell (Morrow, William, & Co.; New York, New York; 1990)

South Africa's War Against Capitalism by Walter Williams (Praeger; New York, New York; 1989)

The State Against Blacks by Walter Williams (New Press; New York, New York; 1982)

Whose Votes Count: Affirmative Action and Minority Voting Rights by Abigail Thernstrom (Harvard University Press; Cambridge, Massachusetts; 1987)

Second Thoughts Project

For more information on the Second Thoughts Project contact:

National Forum Foundation
107 Second Street, N.E.
Washington, D.C. 20002
(202) 543-3515

Contributors

WILLIAM ALLEN is a member of the U.S. Commission on Civil Rights and served as its Chairman from 1987 to 1989. A constitutional scholar, Dr. Allen is also Professor of Government at Harvey Mudd College in Claremont, California. His work has been published in numerous scholarly and other journals.

RICHARD COHEN writes a bi-weekly column for *The Washington Post* and a weekly column for *The Washington Post Magazine*, and is syndicated to 80 other newspapers. As a reporter for *The Post*, he was one of two journalists to break the story of the investigation of then-Vice President Spiro T. Agnew. His book, *A Heartbeat Away*, is about this investigation. Cohen has also written for *Esquire*, *The New Republic*, *Rolling Stone*, *The Nation*, and other magazines and journals.

PETER COLLIER, as Co-Director of The Second Thoughts Project of the National Forum Foundation, also organized the first Second Thoughts Conference in 1987. He later co-edited *Second Thoughts: Former Radicals Look Back at the Sixties*, the collection of papers that came out of that conference. During the 1960's Collier was active in the student movement at Berkeley and co-editor of *Ramparts Magazine*. Mr. Collier has written several books and articles with David Horowitz, including the bestselling *Destructive Generation*, and authored the recently released *The Fondas: A Hollywood Dynasty*. Mr. Collier's essays have appeared in *The Washington Post Magazine*, *Commentary*, *Playboy*, *Fame*, and *Smart*.

STANLEY CROUCH was a jazz critic and staff writer at *The Village Voice* for ten years. His work has appeared in *Esquire* and the *The New York Times*, as well as *The New Republic*, where he was recently named a Contributing Editor. His latest book, *Notes of a Hanging Judge*, is a collection of essays on issues ranging from black middle-class life to the Bernhard Goetz case, black homosexuals, Louis Farrakhan and Spike Lee.

HARMEET DHILLON is a graduate of Dartmouth College, where she was Editor-in-Chief of the *Dartmouth Review*. Her writings have appeared in *Policy Review*, where she was the Assistant Editor, as well as *The Wall Street Journal*. She is currently studing law at the University of Virginia.

HENRY MARK HOLZER has been a professor at Brooklyn Law School since 1982. He is the author of *Sweet Land of Liberty? The Supreme Court and Individual Rights*. Mr. Holzer serves as Special Counsel to the International Society for Animal Rights, the American Foundation for Resistance International, and the Center for the Study of Popular Culture.

DAVID HOROWITZ, Co-Director of The Second Thoughts Project of the National Forum Foundation, organized the first Second Thoughts Conference and co-edited the collection of paper that came out of that conference, *Second Thoughts: Former Radicals Look Back at the Sixties*. During the 1960's, Mr. Horowitz co-edited *Ramparts Magazine*, and authored one of the earliest books on New Left activism, *Student*, as well as several New Left books on U.S. foreign policy, including *The Free World Colossus* and *Empire and Revolution*. Since that time, he has collaborated with Peter Collier on *Destructive Generation*, and numerous other books and essays.

JOE KLEIN is the political correspondent for *New York Magazine*. His essays have also appeared in Esquire and Rolling Stone, as well as other magazines. He is the author of two books, *Payback: Five Marines After Vietnam* and *Woody Guthrie: A Life*.

JULIUS LESTER is a professor of Judaic and Near Eastern Studies at the University of Massachusetts. He has published 17 books, among them *Look Out Whitey! Black Power's Go' Get Your Mama*, and *Lovesong*, an autobiographical account of his conversion to Judaism. Dr. Lester's many essays and reviews have appeared in such publications as *The New York Times*, *New York Times Book Review*, *The Guardian*, *Liberation*, *The Village Voice*, and *The Nation*. A veteran of the Civil Rights Movement, Dr. Lester was a SNCC organizer in the 1960's.

GLENN LOURY teaches political economy at the John F. Kennedy School of Government at Harvard University. His numerous essays have appeared in *Commentary*, *The New Republic*, *The Public Interest*, *The New York Times*, and *The Wall Street Journal*. Professor Loury has been called by the National Journal one of "the 150 national opinion leaders who are making a difference," and by *Esquire Magazine* one of the "men and women under 40 who are changing the nation." He served on the advisory commission for the U.S. Civil Rights Commission and authored *Free At Last? Racial Advocacy in the Post-Civil Rights Era.*

RONALD RADOSH, a Professor of History at the City University of New York, is co-author of *The Rosenberg File*. His early 1960's essay endorsing black nationalism, which appeared in *The Great Society Reader*, marked one of the first attacks on the Great Society from the Left. His subsequent writing has appeared, among other places, in *The New Republic* and *The Wall Street Journal*.

FREDRICK ROBINSON, after studying at Georgia State University, worked for three years for *The Atlanta Journal-Constitution*. As a free-lance writer, his work still appears in *The Atlanta Journal-Constitution*, in addition to the *Northstar News & Analysis*, *Penthouse*, *Catalyst*, *New Dimensions* and *The Atlanta Tribune*. He is also a contributing editor for *Fast Forward*, an Atlanta magazine.

ABIGAIL THERNSTROM is the author of *Whose Votes Count: Affirmative Action and Minority Voting Rights*, which won among other awards the 1988 American Bar Association's Certificate of Merit and the 1987 Anisfield-Wolf Organization Book Award. Her articles have appeared in *The New Republic*, *Commentary*, and other journals. She is a Visiting Lecturer at Boston College and a Senior Fellow at the Pioneer Institute.

JUAN WILLIAMS, for 10 years a reporter for *The Washington Post*, now writes for *The Washington Post Magazine*. He has also published articles in *Fortune*, *The New Republic*, *Atlantic Monthly*, *Harper's*, and other journals of news and opinion. His book, *Eyes on the Prize - America's Civil Rights Years, 1954-1965*, accompanied the PBS television series of the same title.

WALTER WILLIAMS is the John M. Olin Distinguished Professor of Economics at George Mason University. He is the author of numerous journal articles and four books: *All it Takes is Guts*, *The State Against Blacks*, *America: A Minority Viewpoint*, and *South Africa's War Against Capitalism*. A nationally syndicated columnist, Professor Williams also makes frequent appearances on radio and television.